The Balancing Act Priorities of a Social Entrepreneur

Insights on Navigating Life, Livelihood & Legacy

Claudine Reid MBE

Divine Flow Publishing

ISBN: 978-1-9196336-3-3

Layout and Publishing support Divine Flow Publishing Ltd, UK

Cover Design Marie Reid Chrispel Media, UK

As you walk through this book, digesting all the wonderful nuggets of wisdom. Claudine, a woman with great drive, determination and incredible resilience. What actually amazes me is Claudine's ability to dig deep, reflect and press through very challenging times. There are so many lessons to be learnt in life, and this book provides a good breakdown of how to progress and keep moving forward. Claudine has provided insightful directives. Your current trajectory is about to change!!

Charlene Berry - United Kingdom

The book gives a clear balance on how to navigate through life without having to be selfish but instead to practice change with self-care and growth for yourself in order to empower others. It's taught me not to be hard on myself but not to be comfortable with settling for nothing less than doing my best and achieving the most.

Robyn Le Roux - South Africa

This book provides powerful insights into Claudine's inspiring and unique journey, as well as heart-warming lessons through the incredible lens of her experiences. It provides a really welcomed perspective of a social entrepreneur's journey and has so much to teach so many.

School is definitely in session with this book and it gives you so much of what you need to be top of the class!

Yinka Ewuola – United Kingdom

A must-have tool for anyone considering, starting or actually on their entrepreneurial journey! It's filled with knowledge, experience, practical lessons and tips on business as well as valuable insights into the emotional pains, highs, lows, and happiness life throws at you whilst on your entrepreneurial journey. Reading how Claudine balances work, life and faith is inspiring and empowering!

Karen Keane – United Kingdom

The lessons from her life exemplifies faith, strength, resilience, love for people and elegance just to name a few. I believe you will be greatly inspired and your faith spurred after reading this book as much as it did to me.

Olivia Vuadens-Chan – Switzerland

In this book, Claudine is transparent in sharing gems about how she has achieved success in business and life. Getting straight to the point and genuinely wanting to see others win, she does not hold back. This book has given me the courage to continue facing the trials that come my way because success is on the other side."

Gozen Soydag – United Kingdom

A package of inspiration, encouragement and love. It teaches methods to overcome adversity and achieve success in a way that enhances the individual and the communities they live in.

This book particularly addresses women, as we often hold ourselves back from success with the belief that it's not for us. This book should be issued to every young woman to believe in herself and achieve the success she wants from the exact starting point she has.

Stephanie Taylor – Wales

Contents

Foreword by Patrick Reid

It was a ridiculous idea; nobody had done anything like this before, as far as I knew.

Who would really decide to leave a good, well-paid job, with all the flexibility you require, to start a business?

Sometimes life takes you down a particular pathway, which doesn't always make sense. Sometimes it feels absurd, but I've learnt you must trust the process.

My curious efforts ended abruptly when during my research, I found an organisation that was doing exactly what I wanted to do. Discouraged and disheartened, I decided to shelve the idea; until a friend convinced me to breathe life back into the concept. I dug a little deeper and quickly learnt that the organisation in question had overspent on symbols of success and consequently was no longer trading. They overspent on high-performance cars and the like; I was informed that the finance company came to their office to recover the vehicles; they were seen being lifted onto the tow truck one morning, never to be seen again. Now, whilst I believe there is nothing wrong with symbols of success, sometimes those symbols can create a false impression, a little like those who are tied into the social media culture, believing everything that they see over those platforms is real. Be careful; sometimes, things are not always what they seem.

I also quickly learned why the business model, this organisation in question used, was not sustainable and decided to use this key information to support my decision-making process and reshape my idea.

The great lesson learnt was one of Perseverance. Start despite the challenges #doitnow.

I was petrified at the thought of employing strangers; we mainly took referrals from friends and family, people we know, love and trust, which comes with its own set of challenges, but that is another story for another day.

My brother to this day would like to take the credit for recommending a brilliant young lady from his university. She was intelligent and smart, did a phenomenal job organising our administration systems and after a few days it became apparent that she was extremely exceptional. Every time she walked through the door, she brightened the room. She took care of the administration frameworks and rapidly became essential to the office.

Not long after, I had to go away on a family holiday, hugely apprehensive about leaving the business because the last time I went away, there was a significant amount of mismanagement and misappropriation of finances. I decided this time, when I went away, to put everything in the hands of the young lady who had just started, above any other staff member, including my business partner. Everything was left in her care, including the chequebooks, all the passwords, keys and all the financial responsibilities I gave to her.

It created an awkward situation; putting everything in the hands of a junior member of the team, who had only been in the company a couple of months, over my business partner, she did question my decision. Still, I insisted, without going into any details she took the challenge.

I went away with my family and called her now and then to ensure everything was in order. As a founder, one of the key lessons I've had to learn was whom to trust. I could trust her!

I concluded that if I could trust her with my business, I could trust her with my heart. Five months later, I married her.

This was the birth of a lifelong relationship built on love, trust, intellectual stimulation, mutual interests and a fervent love for and trust in God.

Over the next 25-plus years, I have seen my wife evolve into a value-driven, courageous social entrepreneur. She demonstrates this in every area of life, enabling, empowering, and encouraging others, especially women, to increase their capacity to for more. Supporting women to develop social enterprises that add value to communities in the Caribbean, Africa, Europe, the USA, and Asia.

As you turn the pages of this engaging book, you will see some key themes that demonstrate the courage, creditability, and conviction of the author. I encourage you to think about how you can enlarge these key themes in your own way to shape your enterprise and, more importantly, to impact those you have been called to serve.

Claudine demonstrates strength despite challenges, oppositions, competitions, and complications; she takes tasks given to her as if her life depended on it. She is determined to deliver to the highest possible standard that her time, energy and resource will allow.

Collaboration is essential for achievement, and Claudine embodies this. She often reminds our team of the lesson she learnt from one of her mentors – John Maxwell – *"the goal is more important than the role"*. She is well assured within herself and her capability to know that partnership is a continuous process.

Value added – could you put legs, wings or wheels on an idea? As you read, you will see how Claudine demonstrates her ability to add value; whether she is leading a failing school in the capacity as Chair of Governors or Advising one of the largest Banks in the Country to working with grass-roots organisations and faith community leaders or advising the UK government on how they can better support entrepreneurs.

Over the years, Claudine's personal and professional growth has catapulted her into new arenas above what she ever imagined. She has captured elements of her journey in what she sees as the priorities for a female social entrepreneur, promoting balance, poise, grace, courage, and rebellious hope.

Ladies and Gentlemen, I am introducing to the world my queen, who I am proud to call my wife and mother of our two children, the brilliant and phenomenal, Claudine Reid MBE.

Acknowledgments

Let me start by saying Thank you God. I see the evidence of your grace all over my life.

To my amazing husband, my closest friend and cheerleader, your robust confidence in my ability to flourish consistently causes me to increase my capacity for more, your iron sharpens my iron.

Theo and Timone, you are like arrows in my quiver; if I knew you would be this great, we would have made more of you.

My parents are the greatest. Mum, you epitomise radical courage. Dad, you modelled what it means to serve the community. It is literally in my blood.

Mitchell's and Mclean's and everyone in-between, from the roots (our grandparents) to the fruit (us), you all continue to motivate me to take another audacious step.

To every mentor, thank you for leading the way.

To my PJs Community Service family, thank you for allowing me to lead. Your contribution to this part of the journey is priceless. To every client and mentee, you have supported my ability to amplify my voice and my impact.

Aim so high that you will never be bored.

The greatest waste of our natural resource

Is the number of people who never achieve their potential.

Get out of the slow lane, shift into that fast lane.

If you think you can't, you won't.

If you think you can

There is a good chance you will.

Even making the effort will make you feel like a new person.

Reputations are made by searching

For things that can't be done and doing them.

Aim low: Boring

Aim High: Soring

Charles Swindol, Living Above the Level of Mediocrity (1989)

I first came across this poem in 1996 - it was the catalyst to my mindset shift.

Introduction

The pins and needles sensation wasn't really a cause for concern as I was not really in any discomfort. It was the lump that jolted me into action and sent shock waves to my mind and the very fabric of my being. It was the lump that I could not ignore. Subconsciously I knew that something wasn't right. It felt like a defining moment, the first time in my adult life when I had consciously decided that everything else was going to wait because I knew I was in trouble.

It was a warm September I would never forget. The doctor told me to come to the surgery at 5pm. The following eight hours were excruciatingly unbearable; I had 1,001 thoughts rushing through my head. Little did I know that the real pain of anxiety, unease, mental trauma, and distress was yet to come.

After a short examination, the doctor confirmed my worst nightmare. "I am going to refer you to the 2 WW. The 2 Week Wait the UK, National Health Service System to fast track potential breast cancer cases."

I sat in the car for 10 minutes and cried uncontrollably as I tried to make sense of the news I had just heard. Why? Why me? When did this happen? How could this happen? I eat well! I exercise! My Dad died of Pancreatic cancer. Does this mean I am next?

I had grown accustomed to blocking out pain and "just getting on with life". Moving myself further down the priority list was easy. I am the eldest of a blended, non-traditional family. I am a wife, mother, daughter, business owner and community leader. The traits of what psychologists refer to as the older child syndrome are somewhat embedded into the fabric of my being. Reliable, conscientious, structured, cautious, although I hate to admit it, I'm a little obsessive about having a handle on my stuff, with my colour-coded diary and Semi-meticulous time-management system enabling me to be prepared for any eventuality. In contrast, the downside of such notable qualities carries an amount of inflexibility and rigidity. The burden of being a trailblazer carries a level of self-imposed responsibility, potentially rooted in the fear of failure.

I wrote this book because, as a Social Enterprise leader, I wanted to amplify some of the tensions of balancing the important things in life and depending on your age and context, this could include love, livelihood, legacy and leadership.

There is nothing like a life-altering diagnosis to cause you to stop and re-assess, re-view, re-evaluate and re-calibrate. A little like a satellite navigation system (or Global Positioning System, also known as a GPS to my USA friends) gives you a new set of instructions when you have taken a wrong turn. Most drivers will concur that you follow the instructions because you trust the process. You understand that to arrive at your desired destination, the route that you take is sometimes determined by several factors, some of which are completely out of your control.

Have you ever found yourself in a situation where the tension between who you are, what you have to deal with and how you feel about the situation doesn't match up? It feels something like imposter syndrome. That feeling of increased anxiety because you are not 100 per cent sure if this feeling of success is legitimately achieved even though all the data and evidence say that it is. Perhaps like me, you are the one who is in control, structured, and organised, with most things planned at least two to four weeks in advance. There is not much space for spontaneity, and even impulses have to be managed (probably to the dismay of my husband).

The very fibre of my being has taught me that consistency and discipline are key to progress. It is one thing to have a great idea, but it's a completely different thought process to implement a system, strategy and structure to breathe life into that idea.

This book is for you if, like me, you fall into any one of these five categories. You are:

1. A social entrepreneur with a strong missional lead and values-driven approach to problem-solving.
2. Courageous at least 95% of the time, although there are some days when you feel like an imposter.
3. A Leader, either in your home, business, or faith community.
4. Motivated and believe there is more in you, and you desire to increase your capacity for more, although there are some days you are unsure if there is anything more to increase.
5. Empowering others contributes to your satisfaction and personal fulfilment.

In her book "Lost and Found", Sarah Jakes, the daughter of the famous American preacher, teacher, philanthropist, and multi-business owner Bishop TD Jakes wrote, *"if we discuss only our victories and not our struggles, we allow others to believe you can win a war without engaging in battle"*.

This resonates with me because the outward success that so many people see is just a small segment of the story. I will not deny that I have had an amazing life intermixed with some extremely challenging seasons.

"You make life look easy" is the constant message a few of my mentees repeat to me time and time again. Perhaps that is the optimistic child in me. I've adopted the notion of inverse paranoia; it's what Jack Canfield describes as *life being for you instead of against you.*

It's the belief that things will work out for your good.

In the New International Version of the Bible the Apostle Paul that said in his letter to the Romans, "and we know that in all things God works for the good of those who love him, who have been called according to his purpose." This approach has served me well and has allowed me to see things from a different perspective. (Romans 8 Verse 28).

This book shares insights and just ten out of thousands of lessons from my social entrepreneurial journey. The fights experienced range from small to large. They have given me the strength and grace to win and navigate areas of my life. The battles have enabled me to find my way, and in some cases, use my insecurities and personal pain to fuel what I see as the purpose for my life.

Creating coping mechanisms is just one way of enabling your authentic self to walk through the struggles. This fight taught me that just because I have the capacity to help others, doesn't mean I won't ever need help for myself. In the same way I would never tell a police officer that they should never have to dial 9-9-9.

Chapter I

Mind your Business

From the establishment of our first business in 1992 to the development of a new business during the Global Pandemic of 2020 and the several businesses in-between, I have learned to build on top of accumulated experience, knowledge and resources.

The first business PJs Community Service, established by my husband and director Patrick Reid, started out as a grocery home shopping service. With an incredible team of 100 staff and a fleet of 10 vehicles, we were the pioneers of home shopping. Delivering Groceries to 1,000s of vulnerable adults across the London region every week. Based on feedback and demand from our clients, the organisation expanded into homecare service, providing personal and domestic care for vulnerable adults and children.

In 2001, we embarked on a 2-million-pound building project, the purchase and renovation of a 14 thousand-square-foot community facility affectionately known as "Parchmore". This significantly shifted how we conducted business and opened us up to a whole new world of opportunities, networks, and exposure, however, that season is a whole different book for another time.

Whilst the focus and objectives of business may shift, it is important to remain intentional about increasing your capacity for more. This is how you can evolve into the best version of yourself, leading to a profound impact on your business, team, systems, and framework.

To me business has always been about job creation, social mobility and community wealth creation. This gives a longer-term futuristic focus. It speaks more of community transformation and generational impact rather than a quick fix that is, in some cases not sustainable or commercially viable.

As practitioner, consultant and government advisor on social enterprise and social entrepreneurship, I often find myself answering the same questions; how do I grow my social enterprise? What does community transformation look like? How do I develop my leadership skills?

With these questions in mind, I delved deeper into connecting with other social entrepreneurs to form collaborative partnerships and share knowledge. My passion is to equip and empower Social Entrepreneurs across all spheres of influence, to drive economic empowerment and create sustainable Jobs that contribute to community wealth.

What is a Social Enterprise?

According to Social Enterprise UK, a Social Enterprise is a business that:

- has a clear social or environmental mission that is set out in its governing documents.

- is an independent business and earns more than half its income through trading (or is working towards this).

- is controlled or owned in the interests of the social mission.

• reinvests or gives away at least half its profits or surpluses towards a social purpose.

• is transparent about how you operate and the impact that you have.

Social enterprises exist in nearly every sector, from consumer goods to healthcare, community energy to creative agencies, restaurants to facilities management.

Examples include: PJs Community Service, The Big Issue and Divine Chocolate. There are over 100,000 social enterprises throughout the United Kingdom, contributing approximately £60 billion to the economy and employing two million people.

Why do we need social entrepreneurs?

Social Entrepreneurs seek to create Jobs and work opportunities, they seek to bring transformation to the communities they work in, contributing to sustainability. It's business for good, and when they profit, society profits.

Running a Social Business has given me the ability to serve my community, beyond job creation. For over 20 years we made the conscious decision to re-invest our profits into the community by providing training and development opportunities, for young people and families at risk, lone parents, under-served and under-represented founders and faith communities.

It's in my DNA to encourage, enable and empower others. However, the hindrance for some is sometimes the lack of financial resources. I found that if I could create a financial ecosystem that served the community, we would stand a better chance of meeting the overall objective.

The painful question which often helps with a quick reality check is; how could I help someone else if I am unable to help myself? How could I live out a support function, for example, dropping shopping for a parent, topping up someone's utilities, or teaching employability skills if I was not secure myself?

I see business as mission, as a vehicle to demonstrate hope, create jobs, and create opportunities for others to express the highest version of themselves.

More than the money, it is about an ecosystem, intricate layers interwoven around ethics and values. Steered by governmental policy and aided by stakeholders with competing priorities. Driven by curiosity from universities and research bodies, being closely scrutinised by investors, social media and the public at large. Within these complex layers, the tensions of risk management, problem-solving, and creating value in a framework of dis-equilibrium and, on some occasions systemic bias. Apply all of this in an economic, ecological, technological, socio-cultural, legal and political context.

I see money as a vehicle that enables me to do good things in the community without having to feel like I was compromising my values. The ability to create money represents security, opportunity, and insurance, these are some of the tangible elements that marginalised and under-served communities do not see in abundance.

In some cases, the concept of unlearning in order to relearn is paramount to progress. It's relatively easy to give up out-of-date knowledge, much harder to give up unhelpful habits and behaviours. It's perhaps most challenging to unlearn and relearn, our sense of identity, especially as it relates to ideas and concepts that shape our lives and thoughts around - debt management, wealth creation, investment and protection. Again, topics that were not easily accessible in my community and not frequently talked about in underserved communities. As a social entrepreneur, I was cultivating and accumulating skills and knowledge that, on occasion was uncomfortable. However, I had to get comfortable with being in an uncomfortable place. Unlearn what I thought was good and re-learn something great.

Business is important to me; it gives me a sense of freedom.

With the 168-hour allocation of time per week, I was in charge of how I used the allocation. I surrounded myself with the best people that I could connect with and that my resources would allow. I learnt from them and, most importantly implemented the recommendations.

The responsibility of meeting a payroll run every month for 30 years is immense. There were family groups on the payroll; parents and adult children all from the same household. I felt a sense of duty and responsibility to my staff, and I didn't want to let them down.

Minding your business requires you to think about the life cycle of the business and required that I take an agile and flexible approach to the development of the business and even of myself. I believe that as I developed a growth mindset, my business grew because I was intentional, I had an implementation plan, and I was monitoring the impact.

Upon reflection, there is always a better or faster way, but you can only do what you can do at the time. Truth be told, we are running our own race, not in competition or comparison with anyone else.

The key is to stay focused and play your own game.

At each stage of the life cycle of your social enterprise, a different approach is required.

As I have learnt to navigate this landscape, the lessons have shaped my personal development and growth.

It is important for you to understand that when I say lesson one is "Mind your Business" this means:

- take responsibility for what is yours,
- don't believe every thought in your head and
- practise self-awareness.

Reality TV shows have created fortunes from the business of minding other people's business. Social Media influencers build brands almost exclusively on encouraging people to mind *their* business.

What if we took all the consideration, devotion and attention that we focus on other people's lives and applied it to our own business? I think we would have much better outcomes. What if, in doing that, we discovered we have the capacity to transform our communities and cities?

Minding your business gives you more control and increases your impact because you have a more focused approach. This saves you time and energy because you are now investing specifically. Your targeted approach will allow you to be more strategic and deliberate. This strategy will present more learning opportunities because you are clearer about your next steps, enabling you to better support others. Ultimately creating a financial eco-system that allows you to create financial resources.

Michael Jackson's 1988 song "man in the mirror" is the epitome of mind your business. His instruction in the song reminds us that *"If you want to make the world a better place, take a look at yourself and make that change."*

This requires you to take a forensic look at the age and stage of your business, causing you to understand that depending on where your business is, in its evolution, a different strategy will be required. In the same way that in each stage of your life you have applied age-appropriate frameworks and instructions to govern your growth and development.

In the process of the development of my businesses, I have observed there are different stages of the business life cycle, and each stage requires a different strategy;

1. Development & Seed
2. Start-up
3. Growth and establishment
4. Expansion
5. Maturity and
6. Exit

Let's look at the journey from business birth and growth to maturity and decline.

Birth of a Business

Initially, you may see very little return for all the energy and time you put in. Sales are likely to be slow, costs high, with little to no profits. The birthing or introduction stage, whilst this can be a little scary, is a time when your vision, tenacity, and drive come into alignment. It's a little like bringing home a new baby for the first time; everyone in the household is usually excited, attentive and eager to do the right thing with this new life that has joined the family.

In 1992 when Patrick started the business, he invested his redundancy money along with a £5,000 start-up loan from the Prince's Trust (a Charity founded in 1976 by HRH King Charles III to help 18–30-year-olds develop their business ideas.)

This was a time of excitement and drive. With a pioneering approach to business, sometimes you can feel unstoppable, especially when it looks like everything is working in your favour. Patrick, a former British Telecom engineer understood that for the business to be sustainable it was important to ensure standard operating processes that did not centre around himself, but rather around a system, that required skilled and competent people to execute. Late nights and early mornings were the norm as there was a constant desire to find the right pattern or complete outstanding tasks.

When I started my mentoring business in 2020 during the pandemic and whilst I was recovering from breast cancer, I was at a very different place in my life. I had more money and time to invest in research and development. I could detach myself from the expected emotional roller coaster of the business journey. I was certain that I would see a return on my investment, and deep down I wanted a new challenge.

When I joined the business in 1995, I was green. I didn't understand money or investment vehicles. Most decisions were emotionally driven and more focused on what if things went wrong. During the start-up period, I was newly married and a young mum. I was torn between my role as a mother, and a wife, the emotional roller coaster of wanting to be the perfect wife and mother, and the desire for security offered by a robust business. Whilst this is still important to me now, 20 years ago, security was higher on my priority list. Now I have more options for security, and since my portfolio is diverse, I can make investments with a different focus in mind.

During the early stages of development, it is likely that you will be playing multiple roles; your time management and self-care is important. Where possible, invest in a mentor or coach to support your journey. Join a group or network to minimise the feelings of isolation, as you will need this for the next stage.

GROWTH

At the growth stage, sales have begun to increase, and some profit can be seen in the business. Costs are reducing.

The growth stage of a business feels like a teenager with an identity crisis. Experimenting with different hobbies and opportunities to find that sweet spot. Like a teenager, there will be many opportunities presented to you; some may take you off course. The skill of the social entrepreneur is to identify which of those options are closest to the values you want to represent. At this stage, it is very easy to be drawn away to something else and "chase the money" instead of being focused on your core business and purpose.

As a social enterprise, our core has always been to serve the needs of the community. We were very involved in the community and saw first-hand what our involvement meant on a broader, deeper level. We decided to maintain our focus on vulnerable adults and children. Somehow this made sense, there would always be a need regardless of the political agenda, economical focus, technological shifts, social or cultural changes, legal or environmental discussions, this particular client group would always need a service. Now, we had to intentionally build a socially enterprising business model around this concept.

Getting involved with community life was key - serving on local and central government boards allowed us to keep our ears to the ground and implement what we had learned. For example, serving as a school governor and getting involved in charity groups gave us insights into how larger organisations were run. I recall my first government appointment. Totally out of the blue. I received a telephone call from the Education department of the local authority, "we have heard about you and your success; we would like you to take over as chair of governors for Westwood Girls School, which has gone into special measures".

I had more questions than answers.

What do you mean you have heard about me?

100's of thoughts were running wild in my head. Take over a school? I have no idea what you are even talking about, I've worked in a school environment for 12 months as a teaching assistant, and I am very aware that this is not the same thing!

I was excited and apprehensive at the same time. Thrilled and enthusiastic, this was a new opportunity to learn, the chance to impact the education of young people and to create and enhance structures that would impact their future, especially as the school was in a socially deprived area. The examination results were below the national average, teachers and staff had lost morale, and the school had a poor reputation. The prospect of being called in to take over felt like a massive weight of responsibility, hence the trepidation. I had never done this before. What was going to be expected of me? Who do I even know in this space? I didn't know the rules.

Going into an organisation as an outsider allows you to see from a different perspective, there are no emotional attachments. The school was in special measures and I had to hit the ground running. Meetings, meetings and more meetings. The teaching staff, the department for education, academy sponsors, it was all moving so fast, I had documents to read and digest.

The whole experience caused me to grow into a better version of myself. I lead the successful transition of the school into an Academy, appointed a new headteacher, created a more robust financial structure and secured the academic frameworks for an entire school. I improved my negotiation skills, I learnt that things are not always as they seem, there are many power structures at play, and I had to learn about their role in society. More importantly, I saw how I could create improvements in my own business based on the governance structures within the education system.

MATURITY

By now, you are experiencing consistent sales, costs are not as high as at the introductory stage, and there is likely to be an increase in profit.

It was an interesting season when the home-shopping service that was birthed in 1992 came to its maturation. We had known this for a few years, especially when our government contractor would tell us on more than one occasion that after this five-year period, due to the shift in society and the ageing population, shopping would no longer be a compulsory service. We could see the writing on the wall, when this 5-year period was completed there was a strong possibility the contract would not be renewed. Not only would this impact the consistency of the business, but it would directly impact over 30 jobs. However, as social entrepreneurs the maturation of the business allowed us to see opportunities and take a flexible and agile response.

For any new business that we brought on, we were malleable to create an "A Team". Our best driver, shopper and administrator would create a team so the new contracts would get a first-class service. Any challenges or complaints were met with the highest level of professionalism and speed. During the maturity stage, we were able to invest in complimentary services that added value to the overall mission. This is sometimes referred to as forward or backward integration, especially in Manufacturing.

Backward integration refers to the supply chain that happens before your organisation adds value.

Forward integration refers to a part of the process that occurs after you have added value.

Both are strategic opportunities to grow the organisation, reduce costs and increase profits.

The purchase of Parchmore Place in 2001, a 14-thousand square foot derelict warehouse was a turning point in the life of PJ's Community Service, it introduced us to a whole new world. I recall vivid memories of my conversation with Patrick (my husband) about the purchase. Previously we were based on Melfort Road, the third office the business had occupied, slightly off the main, and large enough to accommodate our growing team. We had invited a few friends to come along for a viewing, I was the steady handed camera lady, filming the whole proceeding. I was totally unimpressed. I saw broken concrete, darkness, no lights, no heating, no utilities, trees growing through the broken ceiling, inadequate toilet facilities, neatly packed in stress and darkness.

Patrick saw music recording studios, a thriving multi-functional community space, a children's day nursery and office space. Could we really be looking at the same thing?

PJs Community Service was about 12 years old and was in a mature space to make decisions about its financial future. If we were ever going to impact the community in a significant way, then we had to make this shift.

It took approximately 18 months to sign off on the deal of our life. PJs was mature, and now we have a new baby, a whole dilapidated and derelict building!

Maturity will cause you to see with your mind what others miss with their eyes. Maturity will cause you to delay instant gratification for longer-term values.

Leading a mature business is very different to running a start-up business. I had more to lose. I had emotional attachments, I had invested time, energy, and effort to nurture this thing. At the same time, I was becoming more interested in the leadership development of myself and others. I realised the maturity of the business has a direct correlation to the people that lead and work together.

DECLINE

During this phase you are experiencing reducing sales, constant costs, and reducing profits; it is time to decide if you are going to inject a new lease of life into the business.

It's a hard decision, and I knew what the right thing to do was even before the question was asked. The home-shopping part of the business was way ahead of its time, it was innovative and pioneering, way ahead of the supermarket model, and after 16 years of delivering 1,000 baskets per week of groceries to our clients, the market was taking a rapid nosedive.

Paradoxically, whilst the client group was growing, the funding model required to sustain this business was shrinking. The ageing population in the United Kingdom meant that there were more older people than younger people; this was perfect. However, with increasing vehicle costs, fuel, staffing and training costs, the required expenditure far overshadowed the benefits.

My main concern was the 15 staff working in this section of the business. If we shut down this element of the business, what would happen to the staff? The protracted conversations with Fresh C.M was a massive learning opportunity. It was time to explore how to dispose of an element of our business that was losing money without impacting the other areas of the business.

Some of the team had been with us for over 15 years. Sylvia was there before me, and now I was negotiating the terms and conditions for her transfer.

My business was in decline. Shutting down this element of this business was the safest thing I could do to protect the livelihood and security of my entire team. I felt like a mother telling her child to move out of the family home. I mean, I loved these guys, we had worked together, laughed, and celebrated together, shared the pain of growth and loss together, and now I am responsible for telling them to leave. After the announcement I walked out of the hall, fighting back tears. How on earth am I going to cry in front of the team? It's not like I was forced. It was a clear, calculated, well-thought-out decision to close this chapter.

Hard decisions are your strength. They cause you to see differently and create space for new and bigger opportunities; for as much as we were about to transfer one business, I saw the profitability shift, and it all made sense. The conversation with the accountant gave me a reality check. It's not really about vanity metrics, what determines if an organisation is doing well is numbers that convert into a viable commercial proposition.

Decline speaks of the end and in some cases failure or a re-awakening, a re-positioning, a re-birthing. The opportunity to step into something new and bright. I was excited about the prospects in front of me and anxious about the money at the same time, but I also recognised the landscape had changed and it was time to step into a new mode of operation. I began seeing some of the weaknesses in the business model and could see very clearly why it was necessary to stop collecting cash; the system was no longer fit for purpose, it was outdated and had little technologically investment. As I breathed a sigh of relief, I knew that I was ready for what was next.

- What is the stage of your Business?
- What strategy do you need to employ to increase your weekly and monthly turnover by £2,000, £5,000 or £10,000?
- What strategy do you need to employ to increase the social or environmental impact?
- Identify 5 people that are doing what you are doing. What can you learn from them?

LESSON: Mind your Business

Be clear about your mission, vision and values.

Understand the significant role your enterprise plays in the bigger picture of society.

Realise that at each stage of the lifecycle of your organisation a different strategy may be required.

Chapter 2

Moving beyond the comfort zone

Around 1998 after reading Charles Swindoll's book "Living above the Level of Mediocrity (The poem at the beginning of the book was lifted from his book). I started on a journey to finding myself. I wanted to get into the personal development space but didn't have the finance, the know-how, the access or the understanding of what it would really take.

Silently desperate, I scanned through the bookshelf, searching for help. The words Living above the level of Mediocrity jumped off the page and into the core of who I am. I felt like Mr Swindoll had written the book specifically for me. I knew that there was more in me. I had a sense of purpose, it was part of my DNA. I mean, I am the daughter of Ras. Seymour Mclean, the Book Liberator, the social activist and community champion. That sense of yearning for more, I felt like it was calling me. At this time, I had been married for 2 years and was still getting to grips with what it meant to be a wife and embrace true partnership. I was a mother trying to understand and process the responsibilities of a new life that I was responsible for.

Life felt like a movie that I was starring in but had little control over the outcomes.

I was learning more about myself and getting to grips with understanding that each new season of my life would introduce me to a new version of who I am called to be. Challenging Mediocrity required me to think clearly. It starts in the mind, it is what all successful social entrepreneurs, performance coaches, counsellors and psychologists will tell you. I speak more about techniques I adopt to clear my mind later.

You have to consciously elevate your thoughts and create a new narrative so that you can overcome mediocrity and live differently by seeing with your mind what others miss with their eyes.

I had to learn to combat self-sabotaging habits like; going to bed late and poor eating habits. I had to exterminate the traits that could very easily, and subconsciously hold me captive like; traditionalism, doing things because it has always been done this way and not thinking innovatively for the season of life I was in. Perfectionism would have you stuck to the point of paralysis because everything wasn't flawless. Inflexibility and being closed to new ideas. Now was the time that everything I had learnt from 1998 till now was being tested, could I stand tall? Could I transcend the noise of life?

Moving beyond the comfort zone is a continuous process. You are always moving from one level to the next. These lessons developed an incredible foundation for the next season of life and serve as a constant reminder to explore new things.

The 2021 international women's month theme 'choose to challenge' contributed to enabling me to get started in writing this book. Whilst the theme focused on gender parity, the notion refers to the equal contribution of women and men to every dimension of life. I was focused on what else I could do to challenge my very existence. International Women's Day (8th March) is a global day celebrating the social, economic, cultural, and political achievements of women. The day also marks a call to action for accelerating women's equality. As a leader and social entrepreneur, it is important to me to demonstrate and embody gender parity. Supporting, enabling and celebrating women.

I started by creating the life framework wheel, enabling me to explore the traditions that no longer serve me or my family. A challenged mind is an alert mind. In chapter 11, I speak more about the Life Framework wheel and how you can use it to create the future you and your family deserve.

If I could challenge my thoughts I could challenge my words, if I could challenge my words I could challenge my actions, if I could challenge my actions I could challenge my outcomes. If I could challenge my outcomes I could create new results. New results that would be synonymous with who I was becoming.

In Michelle Obama's best-selling book, Becoming, she spoke of how life has been one of striving, striving to excel as a student, a professional, a mother and the First Lady of the United States. Her story resonates and inspires me, because in the same way she used her influence, drive, and determination to create initiatives that impact women and girls, I aspire to do the same.

Her wisdom and insights gave strength to a woman like me who was on a journey of self-discovery. I was able to look to models of progress and success in our community. A woman that looked like me and strived for a common goal as I did myself.

In the Biblical New Testament account, Timothy was mentored by the Apostle Paul, he was reminded in one of his letters that God had not given him the spirit of fear but of love, power and a sound mind. In stepping out of my comfort zone, my spirit needed to hold onto something bigger than me, because I knew the time would come when; doubt, discouragement and dismay would raise their ugly heads.

When I think of courage, I am reminded of the late great Rosa Parkes and Nelson Mandela. Their audacity and boldness spoke of possibilities. Political leaders of my time, Bernie Grant MP and Diana Abbott MP, demonstrate ground-breaking opportunities to those that dare to step out of the ordinary.

Jennifer Vaugh, the courageous cancer fighter who I met during a support group session hosted by Black Women Rising (a support group for Black Women in the cancer community). Her personal story was a demonstration of nothing less than strength of character, mind, and spirit. Jennifer shared how she had battled with her employers to keep her job whilst living with cancer and knowing the doctors had given her 24 months to live, she wanted to maintain as much normalcy as possible. As I heard her story I could only see her strength and fortitude. I am sure there were moments of anguish, but in that moment, Jennifer epitomised courage, she gave me strength to push harder.

In contrast to strength, stories of fear are also very real, it has the ability to cause dread, terror, anxiety, distress, panic and trepidation. I can recall several occasions on my social enterprise journey when I was held hostage by fear, incapacitated by an inability to move, consumed with worry, which I later learned was a mis-use of the imagination. The fear was usually tied to a feeling of letting people down; my family, my clients, my staff, those that depended on me to get things right.

The chemicals in my brain must have been working overtime; fighting for every thought of fear that would try to consume me. I had to learn to work to combat this by acknowledging the feelings and emotions, understanding how I arrived at this particular place, and reverse engineering the process by nurturing a strong mindset and asking myself what could I do differently next time. I learnt to "do it afraid". I concluded that fear is a legitimate emotion, and part of my responsibility was to learn to embrace and overcome fear and use its energy to propel me to a place of progress.

Going to the Solicitors to update my will and putting a Lasting Power of Attorney in place to cover any eventualities in life felt like stepping out of my comfort zone, as did applying for a role in an organisation with a turnover of in excess of 20 million pounds per year, far above anything I had managed. Writing £50,000 funding application for an organisation. These things had the capacity to pull me out of the comfortable place to explore deeper and wider opportunities.

According to Psychologist Abigail Brenner, there are substantial benefits of stepping out of your comfort zone:

Your real existence exists beyond the bubble of your own personal thoughts, feelings, and beliefs. Your real life is the sum total of all your experiences, not just the ones you're comfortable with. Sometimes it takes a traumatic situation or a major life-changing event to cause you to know that there is life beyond the comfortable place.

Challenging yourself creates the momentum required to push you to dip into and utilize your personal store of untouched, untapped knowledge and resources. You have no idea what you are made of until you venture outside of your own familiar world, into that uncomfortable place.

Taking calculated risks are growth experiences.

Even if you make mistakes or don't get it right the first time, those become experiences you can tap into in the future. There really is no such thing as a "fail" if you get something out of the experience. "FAIL" re-framed is "First Attempt in Learning." The lesson is in the losses. I appreciate this may take time to process, especially in the moment.

Part of your responsibility to yourself is to not settle for the mediocre it's too big a price to pay. Your challenges and risk experiences are cumulative. Every time you try something new and allow yourself to be open to whatever experience arise, you are learning and expanding your repertoire of life skills, self-knowledge and self-awareness. As you do this, you also extend the size of your comfort zone. That is where real growth happens.

Stepping out of your comfort zone ultimately helps you to deal with change in a better way. Life transitions are all about change. Each time you transition, you move to another level. Inevitably, these life transitions transform you.

Advancing through adversity

Crisis can come at any time; COVID-19 has taught us that lesson. Crisis has a way of sobering our daily thoughts. Here we are, trying to pull ourselves together because of a personal crisis whilst observing a global crisis, which has the capacity to have an adverse impact on, not only you and your family, but the entire world.

The mental strain and psychological impact of a breast cancer diagnosis shook me. It took a while to gain a healthier perspective on my situation. There was so much to consider in such a short space of time. How am I supposed to act? What am I supposed to feel? More importantly, how am I supposed to lead? I have a business to run and responsibilities. I have a family. Leading through a crisis has taught me to keep the main thing the main thing. To help myself, I intentionally slowed the pace of my life. The glaring lessons looked like this:

1) make yourself the priority – self-care is a priority

2) educate yourself on key areas where you lack knowledge and understanding

3) be flexible and adaptable - by being open and willing to new concepts and ideas where appropriate

4) leverage the power of the team - invest in a strong, skilful team

5) be authentic – be comfortable with being yourself

Putting myself first was hard because I am used to putting the needs of others before my own; it's a natural instinct. My tendency to put others before myself is natural as a leader, it is what I have done my entire life. I am a responsible, confident, and conscientious person with strong attitudes and beliefs that reflect my parents. Now I was dealing with the tension of knowing who I am and being unable to operate in that role because of my health. On top of that, we were in the middle of navigating our way through a Global Crisis.

I found it helpful to get clarity on "me" and my changing role and needs in my life. By deliberately zoning out from the noise and busyness of life, looking at my emotional, spiritual, mental and physical priorities. It was confusing to process, but I had to keep bringing myself back to context. My context is changing. The things that motivate me are changing, and that is OK.

Find what works for you. You might need the professional services of a counsellor or therapist; that, too, is ok.

Maslow's hierarchy of needs was living out in front of my eyes. Abraham Maslow was an American Psychologist best known for creating a theory of psychological health based on fulfilment. The first human need is for food, water, clothing, sleep, and shelter; basic survival needs. Once these needs are fulfilled, the need for safety and security is next on the priorities, followed by love and belonging, esteem and the pinnacle of self-actualisation.

My physiological, safety, social, and self-esteem needs were met. I thought that my need for self-actualization was being met, and right before my eyes, I could see the shift taking place. I just didn't feel that I was living to the best of my ability. I had settled for safety, and I had become comfortable with the status quo, no longer pushing, no longer striving, no longer living above the level of mediocrity. I felt stagnant. I had not nurtured any new opportunities, which meant that outside of my family, there was not much new to look forward to.

I could see my life and motives changing because of my personal circumstances, which was the difference between life and death.

I found myself going into a time of deep reflection and asking the question:

What parts of my life motivate me to be all I can be, and how will this impact my leadership ability, and more importantly, how will this impact on my health and my ability to move out of the comfort zone where nothing grows?

Life has a new meaning and as I try to navigate my pathway through this uncertainty, I am re-discovering myself. On several occasions I heard my friend Dr. Pearl Jarrett say how she was re-inventing herself in her 50's. I was getting closer to understanding exactly what she was talking about. Pearl, a cancer survivor like me, decided to re-invent herself and DO the things in life that she wanted to do. She joined a modelling agency and starred in some high-profile television adverts. Started several businesses and created a foundation that impacted several countries, sending much-needed medical and education supplies. Most significantly, during the pandemic, her team sourced and sent 2 million face masks worth over half a million pounds to Jamaica.

Life is a series of transitions, and you don't have to stay in the same place forever. That place is the comfort zone. I believe it is "ok" to stay there for a while. However, note that life events cause you to think differently, and by thinking differently, you are likely to start acting differently. You may start to crave different things, for example; bigger goals, more security, and more meaningful exchanges. This is you stepping out of the comfortable place and moving to a better version of yourself, beyond the comfort zone.

LESSON: Beyond the comfort zone

Get comfortable with change and transitions.

Every time you get too comfortable, this is an indication that it is time to stretch and challenge yourself with a new assignment.

Chapter 3

Race, Role Models & Identity

The Equality Act 2010 makes it unlawful in the United Kingdom to discriminate on the grounds of race, colour, nationality, ethnic origin, sexuality and disability and other protected characteristics. Even with legislation in place in 2021 there were still massive discussions about the UK being a racist country and the structures of the country being classed as institutionally racist. As noted in the 1999 Mcpherson report, (commissioned to investigate the murder of Stephen Lawrence, in order to identify lessons learnt in the investigation and prosecution of racially motivated crimes.)

The brutal public murder of George Floyd in the State of Minneapolis, Minnesota, USA, on 25th May 2020 shifted the global conversation about race, racism, diversity, and ethnicity. George Floyd was handcuffed by police officers on the suspicion that he used a fake 20-dollar bill. The police officer, Derek Chauvin, then restrained Mr Floyd by putting his knee on Mr Floyd's neck for nine minutes whilst waiting for police backup. This horrific scene was filmed by members of the public, and it went viral. Members of the general public, some of whom were medical professionals were filmed shouting and pleading with the police officer in question to loosen his grip and help Mr Floyd as he cried, "I can't breathe".

This heinous act led to uproar across the USA and UK as people expressed their anger and frustration over the continuous use of excessive force by police on the black community; without consequences. This was further exacerbated by the countless number of police killings of black people.

Very similar to the notation that Trevor Noah the South African Comedian speaks of in his book "Born a Crime". Being born mixed race in 1984 South African was outlawed. Sex between a black and a white person was illegal!

I saw the images of this when I visited the Nelson Mandela museum in South Africa. It was a tour that rocked me to the very core of my being. There were images of unidentified police officers looking through the windows of people's homes to see if a black person was there. There was a list of laws that black people had to follow. For example, "this beach is for white people only. This rest room is for White people only. A separate water fountain for black people and white people". The fear and anxiety of living under such a regime is difficult for me to process even now in 2022. Even in the criminal justice system, the convicted prisoners were distinguished by the colour of their skin, this would determine how they were treated, how much food they got to eat, the quality of the food and if they could use the bathroom with a full door or half a door.

As Delone, our amazing tour guide, took us through Johannesburg, we saw wealth, poverty and deprivation. "This is the White area, high walls, clean and green. Contrast that with the over-populated tower blocks, littered with empty cans and bottles, people standing around with no jobs and little access to opportunity". Apartheid did this. He explained from his perspective why things are the way they are and what was happening in society.

Closer to home, the inspirational story of the Jamaican-born Len Dyke and Dudley Dryden, men of gargantuan vision, complementary skills and a philosophy that put the needs of building their business above everything else, was the backdrop to which I subscribe. The story of these inspirational entrepreneurs, later joined by their business partner Tony Wade, was captured in the book *How they made a Million, the Dyke & Dryden Story.* It clearly demonstrates that focus and hard work, fortified with resolute determination to succeed is possible.

Life at the best of times can be an uphill struggle, but the colour of our skin as an added consideration seemed unfair. Dyke & Dryden's story tells of an unshakable belief in self-worth, community pride and the struggle to overcome discrimination and prejudice. This is the story of the rise of Britain's biggest Black Owned company and details their ability to overcome barriers to progress, with courageous ambition, drive and philosophy of living.

Growing up, the discussion of racism has been a constant theme in the back of my head, my mother would always remind me that whatever I did I had to be "twice as good, you will be overlooked, you will be ridiculed, no one will take any notice."

It just didn't seem fair that the micro-aggressions I faced was based on the colour of my skin. So, if I wasn't black, how easy would life be? It's not something I wished for, but it is a question that ran through my mind.

As a black female social entrepreneur, I have always been mindful that in most rooms, I am the minority. There are not many people that look like me in the spaces where I operate. I am usually the trailblazer. I took on the responsibility and feeling of having to make "social enterprise" work, not only for myself but for the next generation.

Knowing that advancement is attainable is key to making significant progress.

Role models inspire the journey. There is something unique about seeing someone that looks like you achieve the success that you are striving for. Whilst it doesn't take away the lessons from the journey, from a psychological perspective, it demonstrates what is achievable. And the power of visualisation teaches that if the mind can see it, you can strive to work towards it.

As a Black, British, happily married, Christian woman, there are several categories of underrepresentation that I very easily fit into.

My childhood home was in an area named the "American Estate". As many of the roads were named after several states in America. I come from a lone-parent household; my amazing mother did her absolute best to provide for my younger brother, 12 years my junior She had a part-time job. When the relationship with her then husband broke down, her meagre wages were not enough to cover the mortgage on the beautiful three-bedroom semi-detached property.

She informed me that the bailiffs were coming to repossess our house, and after school I was to call her from a telephone box, and she would tell me where we would be sleeping that night. It makes sense now; she had called my uncles a few days before to remove our sofa suite and TV and put them in my grans basement out of the glare of the debt collectors. So, when they came to the house our possessions would not be in their glare. I was living this experience as a 15 year old girl, I didn't really understand the impact of this season of my life, it was shaping who I was becoming. Here was a strong black woman, my mother, navigating her way through a traumatic relationship breakdown, being made homeless with two dependants, and on a part time income. An experience that I learned later in life would shape my outlook on motherhood, marriage, financial management and faith.

During this time, I started to mentally make some key decisions about my life, such as where I wanted to go, who I wanted to be and how I wanted to live. I never wanted to be dependent on anyone, least of all a man who said he loved me then ran off with someone else. I had to ensure that the decision that I made in my 20's would start to shape my destiny.

It's the reinforcing message that National Sales Director and Independent Consultant Crisette Ellis from Detroit, USA, taught me. A significant influence and mentor in my life. Crisette, to me, is a devoted wife and mother, she is beautiful, elegant, and smart, she is a courageous leader and inspirational role model; her business acumen is top class.

On one of her many trips to London, I recall a shopping trip to Central London, as I saw the cashier totalling up the bill, my eyes widened; that was my mortgage payment for 6 months that she had spent in one shop. I asked without hesitation, why did you spend so much money? Her response would catapult me into another stratosphere of thinking "I made decisions in my 20's and 30's that would allow me to live a life of financial freedom". Crisette not only talked the talk, but she walked the walk. This was clearly demonstrated in her business acumen and rewards.

I immediately decided to review my financial roadmap and portfolio.

Our children are raised in a traditional Christian home; warm, loving and compassionate. Family is priority, laughter is medicine and my husband Patrick's chicken soup has healing properties. Family conferences are how we solve problems, money is a vehicle, we prudently share it and use it as a defence as instructed by the old-testament scripture. We use money but we don't love it. We were intentional about exposing our children to opportunities that we never had at their age. They went on international school trips, when we were out of the country they boarded at school. They took part in extracurricular activities at least two or three times per week and took part in sporting fixtures and activities at the weekend.

They grew up seeing us as pillars in the community, providing jobs for thousands of people. The purchase of our first commercial property in 2001 was a massive turning point in our family home. The property affectionately known as "Parchmore" become our extended front room. Everyday after school we stopped there on the way home. My children saw leadership, ownership and responsibility. Of course, all of this comes with a price, that I wasn't aware of yet.

We were raising children that have a different set of expectations about life than what we had. The very thing that made me who I am, Bishop TD Jakes refers to it as *"the struggle is the very thing that we have tried to protect our children from"*.

In carving out a particular type of lifestyle and pushing myself to strive for more, bigger, and better. It shielded my children from some of the encounters that I had. Not being able to go on international holidays, and not having the latest electronic games or the latest trainers, all material items that are of key importance to young people of this generation. We were able to provide this.

We had established a vehicle, a business model that was robust, that didn't rely on us for its day-to-day operational success. Our children did not see the barriers or the racism we experienced. But rather they experience freedom and opportunity of a higher grade. They never once came home and reported that a teacher had made a racist remark, like I told my mum when my Physical Education teacher said to me; "there you go Claudine, I said it in Jungle language so you could understand!"

Patrick and I were driven by social impact and community transformation. When Dr Tariq Shabeer, an officer of the local council, introduced the concept of social enterprise it was received with a warm welcome. He helped us see how what we were building was in line with the government policy. He helped us to crystallise our thoughts and take our thinking from a community focus to a more regional and national focus encouraging activity in community life and to better understand the power structures that govern society. Watching on the side lines were our children observing with a keen eye, how their parents were growing.

Dr Tariq Shabeer enabled and facilitated some of the opportunities that I thought were impossible. God in Business Conference at Croydon Town Hall was a major turning point, my first event with over 150 attendees, this partnership project with a US based organisation thrust us into the limelight. I had no idea of my capability or capacity to host a conference of this magnitude in the Town Hall. I doubted my ability to manage an international team, I questioned my ability to lead a media campaign to stimulate participation, that required attendees to actually pay money to attend, more importantly I had not done this before, and they were expecting me to lead it. I had no one to look up to for help.

As daunting as it felt, I blazed the trail with the first of many successful international events and conferences. It felt like a rebirth; it felt like I was being introduced to a new version of life, and more importantly, I was able to respond. I could do this because I am black, because I can connect with my community, and because I am a Leader. Beneath the façade of strength, courage and progress, I could connect with my community because I understood the anxiety and apprehension that comes with stepping outside of the imposed normal. The challenges of the unknown and the fear of having no backup plan. The exciting aspirations for the future of your family but not seeing it done enough to believe that it is attainable and within your grasp. I had accumulated a level of skill, knowledge, discipline and resource to help myself and also to help others to go a step further.

It's that backdrop that makes me ask the question about; identity, role models and the importance of representation. I believe representation is important because it gives individuals the freedom to be themselves without having to conform to a set of codes that do not reflect them or their cultural identity or social class.

Many black people refused to be defined by the circumstances of their past or by their challenging life experiences. I choose to refuse to be incarcerated by negative, self-limiting thoughts and a lack of role models that look like me.

I choose to take a path that blazed my own trail. This started with the concept of self-talk also known as positive affirmations. I choose to tell myself everyday who I am, what role I play and the impact of my actions. This has a profound positive impact on my mental and spiritual well-being. Even effecting my posture and habits. This means you can't just say it. You have to act like it. I practise saying out loud:

"I am **Courageous**"

I focus on conquering the challenges of life.

If there is a challenge, my usual disposition is to retreat into my space alone to think it through. In that space of thinking, I find emotional and spiritual strength, power, and boldness. I am open to inviting others into that space in order to help myself increase my capacity for more or even move past that stuck or comfortable place.

"I am a **Leader"**

I demonstrate love through servant leadership.

I am usually the individual heading up organisations, committees, and companies bringing a sense of stability, structure and system in order to contribute to the success framework.

"I am **Audacious"**

I have a bold, fearless approach.

I am a calculated risk taker. It was Sir Richard Branson that said, "*if you see or are given an opportunity, say yes and figure out how to do it later*". I enjoy doing new things that stretch me and take me out of my comfort zone.

"I am **Understanding**"

My personal values and beliefs are rooted in the Christian faith.

I believe it gives me the compassion and empathy required to understand perspectives and appreciate life from someone else's position and perspective, even if we have opposing views.

"I am **Determined**"

Guided by purpose, this helps me to stay focused and driven. I am organised and meticulous with my time. I believe that my determination causes me to practice possibility thinking.

"I am **Innovative**"

With a solution-focused mindset. I enjoy new experiences and getting under the skin of new ideas, it creates metaphors for life and living and shows me how to adopt a pioneering, trail-blazing approach.

"I am **Nurturing**"

It is where I get a percentage of personal fulfilment as a community and business leader. That no-nonsense, confident approach to life. My life has had a number of colourful, non-conventional experiences, which I believe have taught me unique ways to navigate life and forge my path.

"I am **Empowering**"

Using the vehicle of care, education, and social enterprise support to empower others. I am intentionally enabling people to increase their capacity for more.

I have always been an employer, never an employee, so my viewpoint is based on my real lived experience and sometimes, when I hear the experiences of others, I am stunned.

I didn't realise the impact and the privilege that being a business owner had afforded, me.

- The time and freedom.
- The opportunity to work where I wanted.
- The opportunity to create generational wealth.
- The opportunity to see social mobility in action.
- Being present for my children.
- Being able to build something that was based on my personal values.
- Being able to live my purpose through my work.
- Being responsible for my personal growth.
- Being responsible for creating over 9,000 jobs.
- Leading a team of incredible movers and shakers.

Caveat that with the stressors of:

- Managing people, especially when they are having their own personal struggles.
- Debtors not paying you on time.
- Having to use your personal funds to prop up the business.
- Having to re-mortgage a property to cover a massive tax liability.
- Balancing a TUPE transfer.
- Being responsible for family groups that are on the payroll.

- Looking into the future and creating what you want to see with the limited knowledge, resources, talent, and access you have.

I came to a natural deduction that life is a series of experiences. Every experience introduces you to a new version of yourself. Enabling you to step out of the comfortable place and navigate a world of insecurity, challenge and fear of the unknown. In doing so, you are subconsciously telling the world and, more importantly, telling yourself that you are stretching, just like that rubber band, it is at its best when it is being stretched.

The fabric of who we are is made up of experiences, stories, and the symbols we hold dear.

The concept of Head, Heart, Hand and Habits was a guiding principle I adopted from the author Ken Blanchard, most famous for the one-minute manager series of books.

It captures the essence of life and how you use your:

- Head to gain strategic advantage and lead yourself
- Heart to maintain a connection with people and to lead others
- Hands focus on what you do on a tactical, operational level and
- Habits speak of how you replenish yourself to maintain a healthier perspective

I'm still trying to determine if I have what Psychologists call bootstrap mentality, where you are able to pull yourself up and out of a situation; for one person, this can serve well, but for another, this may not be the case.

- Race, Role Models and a sense of belonging that comes with knowing who you are, feel like pieces of a jigsaw puzzle. Each piece is critical to your personal and professional growth. Each piece is shaping you for the next season of your life.
- Are you able to identify at this stage what those pieces are and the significance of the contribution?

LESSON: Race, Role Models & Identity – life is what you make it.

Representation is key to personal and professional development. Being able to identify with history reminds you where you have come from, seeing others achieve what you want to accomplish creates a vocabulary of overcoming incredible odds, it has the capacity to strengthen your mindset and position yourself to accumulate the skills required to proceed to the next level.

Chapter 4

The F Word

Experiencing the downside of life is always a sobering and humbling process; it's a time to pause and reflect. An opportunity for the lesson to catch up with you. It is a time for you to think and evaluate the outcomes.

I like to remind myself:

- Failure is an event, not a person.
- Failure is not final.
- Failure is part of the process.
- It is an important component of the success equation.
- Even though I believed this to be true, the last few years, in particular have reaffirmed this reality.

To get to the desired goal there are bound to be some mistakes along the way, perhaps some errors of judgement, some hard lessons that showed my lack of knowledge, money, mismatched priorities and even floors in my emotional development. My skill was to learn how to use those mistakes as lessons to build the muscle of my mind, my emotions, and boost my capacity for more.

Society has cast a massive frown on failure; it almost feels like everything has to be perfect and if it is not, then you are not a good enough contributor. This damaging message does allow for learning or for the personal and professional growth that happens in this space. That is one of the reasons I believe mentors, coaches and accountability partners are important for progress.

Some cultures have not taught us to view failure as part of the success equation taking you closer to your goal. However, I have also learnt that every failure has introduced me to a different version of who I am. This was not such a bad thing, because I was learning to find my strength in the challenges of life. It felt like it was part of the process. New lessons, develop a new level of understanding, new thinking strategies, new hope, and even new dreams. Failure helped me shape a better and stronger understanding of the things that I didn't want, just as much as it helped me form a clearer perspective of what I did want.

Failure helped to develop the muscle of my courage and allowed me to see things from a different viewpoint. Your circumstances and your options look very different when you feel like you are on the floor of life.

In 2013 I stepped into the political arena and decided to stand to be a local councillor. I had begun to immerse myself in the political arena, organising the hugely successful God in Government event https://www.youtube.com/watch?v=neJhFvzJiW8 at the House of Parliament with MP for Newham Steven Timms, Chair of Christians on the left Andy Flanagan, and my Mentor Pastor Celia Collins.

It was a deeply fulfilling moment in my experience, leading my community to a deeper understanding of what civic engagement looked like and, more importantly, the impact and implications of the engagement on wider society. I was determined to stand in front of the faith community to demonstrate how to use the motivation of faith to serve society. This was actually bigger than me. I was surrounded by a great team of experienced and wise individuals, all putting significant confidence in my ability to represent.

By the time I completed the application and interview process, my credentials were looking good. I had enough evidence and excellent results to articulate my desire and my drive. I was committed to social justice and equity. I volunteered as a school governor for three years, lead a number of local and regional events, and worked with senior MPs on national programs, I was getting ready to represent the Social Enterprise movement in South Korea. I was responsible for creating thousands of jobs in the local community.

My first unsuccessful attempt taught me how to answer questions and think on my feet. I was standing in a room of people that did not look like me, but I understood their drive for significance and progress. I was hesitant about whether I could truly represent them. But I pressed through.

My second, third and fourth attempts strengthened my vocabulary, allowing me to think about society and the bigger picture and how the respective structures within the community converge. I was learning about power structures and understanding the role of Business, Culture, Media and Faith and how these vital pillars of influence in society contribute to an equitable society.

It was whilst hosting the conference where the late great Bahamian Teacher, Preacher and World Changer Dr Myles Munroe was a guest speaker that I was about to learn one of my greatest leadership insights. I took pleasure in serving on the administration team at this event. I was in the green room organising. My mentor, Pastor Ceila, who happened to be Dr Munroe's Mentee said to me, "practise your speech right now, let Dr Myles help you."

I was not ready! I did not have my notes! This was not speech time! Nevertheless, I thought about the opportunity, gathered all the courage I could muster and shared my speech.

"Sit down" he said, I was about to be coached by one of the greatest leaders of our time on how to speak to power. *"Every time you speak you must include the next generation, it will widen your vision and give it life. It will demonstrate your ability to think into the future and then ask the question, what will this mean in ten* years' *time? How will this impact the economy? What could the political landscape look like? What social or cultural trends in society will have shifted?* What *is the impact of technology, machine learning, artificial intelligence and data management? To what extent does this address the issues around net carbon zero?* What *are the legal or policy implications on a Community, City, County or Continent?"*

Those words were power and have never left me. I began to reshape the way I thought, not only about politics but also about my social enterprise and its impact on wider society. That short conversation had a massive ripple effect, and a few weeks later, on my fifth attempt, I won the vote to stand to be a councillor in Croham Ward elections.

Whilst I did not win the actual seat to become an actual councillor, the process taught me about community and leadership, and it demonstrated how the community works either for you or against you. I saw why some communities prosper and why some do not. I saw why the schools in the south of the borough were more prosperous. I gained insights about the health inequality experienced by those living in the North of the borough and how just by reason of your postcode your life expectancy could decrease by ten years. The statistics were alarming. But what was worst was the continuous cycle of deprivation with no real end in view. Yet whilst politicians were speaking of change, nothing really seemed to be changing. At any one time, even the best of ideas had at least 50 per cent of voters opposing them.

Upon deep reflection, I'm not sure if I really wanted to be a politician or if I just wanted to do something different during that period of my life. Perhaps this was a learning exercise. It felt like there were way too many strings attached, and I couldn't really lead in the way that I had grown accustomed. Politics to me, didn't feel heartfelt, making promises to people that you have no idea if you can fulfil because you are at the mercy of the opposition, fighting to ensure your ideas do not come to fruition. Is this really about the greater good for the people or about self-serving, self-interest? I could not reconcile this new way, and after the local election, I abruptly ended that season of my life.

It is important to note that the end of this season was because I could see further and bigger than where I currently was. This was not like the failure of my driving test passed on the third time; after realising you cannot just blag your way through, you actually have to study and engage your brain. This was not like failing my maths examination, I realised that after three failed attempts, I would have to find another way.Neither was this like failing to win a contract that I had worked so hard to secure, only to receive the perfectly typed email that read; we regret to inform you that your application has been unsuccessful on this occasion. This was not even as soul-destroying as losing a childhood friend that, in your youthful innocence, thought you would be friends for life. It felt more like a natural conclusion, a genuine ending to a season.

In the same way that when the season shifts from Winter to Spring, a new set of instructions are required for this important transition. In the winter we make snow people or go ice skating, we wear warmer clothes. In the Spring, we may choose to change our wardrobe, walk more or engage in spending more time inopen spaces. . When the season changes, we take it as done. We are now ready for what's next.

The place in-between your ending and your next is a place for reflection, examination and deep thought. I believe this is where growth happens. It is your space where you allow the lesson to catch up with you. It is a place to learn about yourself. You get the opportunity to ask some reflective questions.

The purpose of the reflective questions is to prepare you for the next level of living. It is like each failure or obstacle teaches you to get tough with life and sharpen your strategic thinking capabilities. This may mean you have to educate yourself, read more books or listen to audios. It may mean aligning yourself with a coach or mentor that will hold you accountable to keep the promises that you made to your future self.

Reflective questions teach you to face everything and rise, rather than retreating into a corner and deciding to never try again. We adopt the philosophy of the contemporary RnB artist Aaliyah's Song "Try Again".

I learnt the art of focused self-refection in my quiet times. I gave myself permission to block out time to think and reflect. Armed with a journal and coloured felt tip pens, I would force myself to think about one key issue at a time. This was not an easy task. I wear several hats, wife, mother, and social entrepreneur; at any given time, there are several hundred thoughts running through my mind, all with differing and competing priorities. Once focussed, I would map out illustrations that capture my thoughts and intentions. Once captured in my journal, I would date my thoughts to allow myself to reflect on the growth journey.

Focused self-reflection allows you to plot out an alternative pathway. If I had the opportunity to do this again, what would I do differently? According to counsellors, this requires a deeper level of interest, curiosity, inquiry, and in some cases, compassion. Specifically, when exploring feelings, thoughts, conduct or performance and reactions. Notice exactly what you are feeling in your body, experiencing in your emotions, and thinking in your mind; this will allow you to make an informed decision as to how you want to act in the future and put coping mechanisms in place to enable the new and improved you to navigate the failures of life.

Depending on your context I want to be careful to remind you that there is not a one size fits all approach and it is likely that you may need to try several strategies until you find the right one that works for you.

- Failure taught me that sometimes you don't really know how strong you are, until being strong is your only option. What has failure taught you?

LESSON: The F word

Failure is part of the success equation it is part of the process, every failure is a lesson and will introduce you to a different version of yourself it is a stepping stone to the next opportunity.

Chapter 5

Accountability is Key

It became more noticeable on my 40th birthday, perhaps because I was in reflection mode. Four decades is a long time. I realised that the pouch, also known as fat, that was gathering around my middle was not moving. I could very easily justify this; I have two children. It's the default position of many women my age. But in addition to the pouch, I struggled to walk up a hill and got out of breath too quickly for my liking. I had horror visions of me not being around because of my poor health and, most importantly, not taking the responsibility to look after myself. I had buried myself in my social mission. It was an easy thing to do. The feeling of fulfilment that comes with seeing others rise, creating frameworks of support that contribute to job creation and financial sustainability.

Knowing what to do is one thing but doing the thing that you know you should be doing is a whole different ball game. Like many people, the law of diminishing intent started to set in. The law of diminishing intent says, "the more you intend to do something, the less likely you are to actually do it."

It was time to get serious!

One of the techniques that I have adopted in my life is to live intentionally by connecting with people that are doing what I want to do. Sometimes those people are very much in our space, but we do not recognise the role or contribution they make, because of the lens that we are looking through. Another way to think about this is accountability.

When you are personally accountable, you take ownership of circumstances and conditions that you are involved in. You see them through, and you take responsibility for what happens, the good, bad and the ugly.

Accountability speaks of a situation where an individual or organisation holds responsibility for the outcome of an activity. For example, you may be accountable for managing a department in your place of work or organisation. Or you may be accountable for ensuring a sum of money is collected, you are answerable for the desired outcome. Therefore, to help myself, I made myself accountable to someone that I respected, someone that demonstrated the results that I wanted to achieve and someone that was able to exhibit the habits and personal success criteria that I was trying to develop.

That person was my younger brother. The timing was perfect, I told him of my intention, and he told me he had just decided to return to the gym and to take immediate action by signing up to C28 with Personal Fitness trainer Issac Morrision. C28 was a 28-day fitness challenge. Focusing on physical fitness and nutrition. The conditions were shaping up nicely. To further help myself. I asked Ryan every morning for 2 weeks of the program to pick me up from home so we could go together. At the time, I wasn't sure if he even realised the impact of what this would do for my productivity, but in requesting him to pick me up meant that I was cancelling the excuses like; its cold, I'm tired, I can't be bothered, I just don't feel like it, I have no energy today.

I didn't want to let him down. But more importantly, I didn't want to let myself down (read that line again). I've learnt that it is harder to keep the promises you make to yourself than it is to other people. I wanted to show him I was disciplined and that I could do this. In my mind, I had subconsciously told myself I am accountable to Ryan, and I knew that if I cancelled for any reason, he would challenge my reason; that was the other thing, he wasn't a pushover.

As I started the 6am training routine, I enjoyed the newfound camaraderie and the challenge with the others in the group. Everyone had their own personal goal that they were striving towards. Everyone had their own personal motivation, and rather than competing with each other, we were competing with yesterday's goal. By the end of the month, the habit was set. James Clear, author of Atomic Habits, suggests that a small change in your behaviour will not transform your life overnight. But if you are able to turn that behaviour into a habit that you perform daily it will lead to massive changes.

Changing your life is not necessarily about making big breakthroughs or revolutionizing everything you do. It is more about building a positive system of habits that, when combined, deliver remarkable results.

I already felt physically and mentally stronger, there was an extra bounce in my step. The pouch at the front felt different, it happened because I was intentional about my progress, I was accountable to someone that I respected enough for their opinion to count. Accountability requires transparency; it requires you to be truthful about the status quo, and setting yourself up for success also means coming out of your comfort zone, which will require an element of stretch.

The impact of going to the gym at 6am set me on a new pathway. The experience of learning and discovering new abilities, pushing and challenging myself past self-imposed limitations, created new neurological pathways in my brain. I could see the impact that this was having in other areas of my life, including the way I was thinking.

"Push past the way you feel", I would tell myself in the morning when my duvet wanted me to stay. Sometimes you have to position yourself to listen to logic and not feelings. It is easy to break the promise you make to yourself, and that is one of the reasons why accountability is key. Progress is hardly ever linear, this teaches that consistency is king, even on days when you don't feel like it. Over time it wasn't that the weights I was lifting were getting lighter 70 kilograms will always be 70 kilograms. One mile will always be one mile. It never gets lighter or easier. I was getting stronger, and I could very easily apply this same philosophy to my business. I had a goal and an accountability partner, most importantly, I decided to make it work.

During this season of my life, I adopted the S.A.V.E.R.S principle that Hal Elrod speaks of in his book 'The Miracle Morning'. The concept of the miracle morning subscribes to the notion that having a good morning routine sets the tone for a fulfilling and progressive day, leading to a positive effect on your general well-being, because successful days lead to successful weeks, successful weeks lead to successful months. Successful months lead to successful years.

This framework helped me to establish a routine that was conducive to where I wanted to be. The recommendation was to fit the framework into an hour in the morning by assigning a timeframe to each of the following activities. I found that as I got into the routine, I adjusted the times for each activity and even doubled up on some activities to maximise the benefit, this led to clarity of vision and thought, less overwhelm and more focus.

Silence

(Prayer or meditation) use this time to connect with God. It will cultivate a deeper level of spiritual **strength**, bring more **balance** to your life, clear your mind, and connect you with a deeper sense of purpose.

Affirmation

An affirmation is a positive statement used to encourage, motivate, and uplift yourself or others. I was already convinced about the power of affirmations. I needed something that I wouldn't forget. The letters that spelt my name was the perfect choice. I assigned a positive, motivating, encouraging word that would speak life to who I was becoming.

Visualisation

Visualisation is a technique used by many world-class athletes. It is the practice of seeing your world how you want it to be seen by consciously and intentionally changing your thoughts and using your imagination to experience new behaviours. By taking one event at a time and seeing yourself win, feeling that jubilation, and creating that sense of achievement, and accomplishment, will allow you to take the real action that is synonymous with the actual win.

Exercise

Physical Exercise has the capacity to not only impact your body but also your mind. As I got into my one-hour fitness class with Meso Fitness instructors, I could feel my strength growing. I adopted the theme for the year of "capacity for more", and every morning I reminded myself that I was "Increasing my capacity for more" this was a great reminder and strength builder, especially on those days when my body was trying to tell me to skip a day.

Reading

I had set myself the audacious ambitious goal of reading 52 books in the year. In real terms it worked out to be 24 books for that particular year. It felt like I could feel my brain growing. To help me remember in some cases I would draw diagrams of the concepts that I had read in order to help me to remember and file the new knowledge that I was consuming. The rational to learn more, read more came from the drive to increase my mental capacity. I wanted the knowledge, I wanted to improve myself, and the least expensive way to do that was to make time for reading.

Scribing (writing/journaling)

I became more intentional about what I wrote and used this as an opportunity to express my emotions, fears, concerns as well as my joys and celebrations. The incredible thing was, at different instances I would re-read my thoughts, I could see growth, progress and sometimes stupidity.

Resilience

According to the American Psychological Association

Resilience is an incredible muscle.

"The process of adapting well in the face of adversity, trauma, tragedy, threats or significant sources of stress — such as family and relationship problems, serious health problems or workplace and financial stressors. It means "bouncing back from difficult experiences."

Evaluating the vicissitudes of life requires you to build muscle not only physically but also mentally, emotionally, spiritually, and intellectually.

Mindset routines and development play an important part in your progress steps, reinforcing the idea about your thoughts and how integral this is to your progress. If you think you can or if you think you can't, either way, you are right.

What you focus on will flourish, the key to success is consistency. Consistency is more important than perfection. If you want to be taken seriously, be consistent. I accumulated small but consistent habits that ultimately led to the results that were unimaginable when I started. Success and progress as a social entrepreneur is more about consistency.

Consistent smart work that leads to success. If you are persistent, you will get it. If you are consistent you will keep it. Consistent action creates consistent results. Part of courage is simply consistency it's not what we do once in a while that shapes our lives it's what we do consistently. Discipline is about consistent action it's about effort, when you bring that effort every single day that is where transformation happens that is how change occurs. Trust is built with consistency, it will outlast short-term intensity.

What you do everyday matters more than what you do once in a while. Dreams come true when you are awakened to the situation and work on it with consistency.

I am at an age where I am only interested in consistency, stability, respect and, loyalty. A leader in sports, business, or any other field of endeavour should possess and provide the same qualities inherent in a good parent. Character consistently depends on ability, accountability, knowledge, good judgement, respect, courage, discipline, fairness, and structured consistency. It's the relentless commitment to consistency that, like raindrops, creates a hole in the rock not because of its strength but because of its consistency. Whatever is difficult can be done with regular attendance, attention and action. Find your speed and pace, and maintain your velocity.

Consistency engenders stability, this will bridge the gap from where you are to where you want to be. Everything you want is waiting for you on the other side of consistency.

It was Dr Cindy Trimm's book, the Soul Fast, that helped to shape my personal and spiritual routines. Soul Fast is a concept that encourages the reader to think more about what is eating you. It is the emotional patterns of life that we neglect and often goes unresolved. Those patterns have the capacity to hinder progress and create unresolved issues that are responsible for derailing progress and leveraging opportunities.

Sometimes we can get lost in the dance of life. I found that taking a deep, soul-searching, introspective look at my thoughts helped me develop the discipline and consistency required to make holistic progress in the unseen areas that matter the most.

- Accountability separates the wishers in life from the action takers that care enough about their future to take responsibility for their daily actions.
- What frameworks of accountability do you hold yourself up to?

LESSON: Accountability is Key

Accountability requires a higher level of thinking and produces a higher level of results, which can ultimately be measured and monitored.

Chapter 6

Mustard seed faith

The Oxford Dictionary defines faith as:

1. complete trust or confidence in someone or something.
2. strong belief in the doctrines of a religion, based on spiritual conviction rather than proof

In the Amplified version of the Gospel according to St Luke chapter 17 verse 5 and 6 the account is told about the parable of the mustard seed:

> 5 The apostles said to the Lord, "Increase our faith [our ability to confidently trust in God and in His power]."
> 6 And the Lord said, "If you [a] have [confident, abiding] faith in God [even as small] as a mustard seed, you could say to this mulberry tree [which has very strong roots], 'Be pulled up by the roots and be planted in the sea'; and [if the request was

> in agreement with the will of God] it would have obeyed you.

The powerful message conveyed in this parable is that you have faith, the size of a mustard seed. You can do great things.

The mustard seed is the smallest of seeds, that grew into a huge plant. In other words, regardless of the size of your faith even if it is as small as a mustard seed as long as you have strong roots and you are grounded in a confidence that is bigger than yourself, you are able to do more than you can think, ask or even image when you take action steps towards the desired goal.

In his book "Living above the level of Mediocrity" by Charles Swindoll he describes what it takes to confront, overcome, combat and resist mediocrity. As I immersed myself deeper in self-reflection, I began to recognise the shift in my thinking and the role that faith plays in the journey of life.

I could feel the muscle of my faith expanding. My internal and emotional muscles were increasing; it was becoming easier for me to set priorities as well as respond to hard questions. The dragon of traditionalism was being slayed, and my internal battles over low self-esteem and imposter syndrome were being fought. All converging to a point that allowed me to give myself the permission to stand tall when tested, stand firm when feeling disheartened, and stand strong when tempted.

Over the years, we have hosted a number of international delegates, in particular Shanghai, Finland and Wales. The guests were usually part of a social enterprise learning tour that wanted to explore our model of progression and development in this sector. "What motivates you? " Was one of the questions the interpreter asked in an interview with a delegation of five businessmen that came from Shanghai to observe and learn from the success of our Social Enterprise Model.

"Why do you serve the community in this way?"

How could I respond in a way that maintained my respect as an award-winning social entrepreneur, without sounding like a fanatical, delirious, black woman, having no understanding of the political, economic, or social constructs that contribute and govern the way how we live?

I carefully processed the question and responded something like this: "I believe leadership is about service, it's my outward demonstration of what is on the inside."

"How noble and honourable", they replied through the translator.

My truth is that I was not actually looking for honour. I was motivated by something intrinsic, something bigger than myself, that spirit filled sense of purpose, consciousness that good must prevail, and de-privatising that internal drive using the vehicle of social enterprise, care and empowerment put a missional focus on my internal drivers that allowed my faith and focus to become tangible. I consciously focused on intentionally increasing my capacity for more, by creating and implementing solutions that impact under-served and marginalised communities.

It's a tense conversation that I have had on many occasions with women in particular that are challenged by the conflict of faith and their version of success. If God wants me to be successful, it will fall into my hands. I am both challenged and concerned by this school of thought. Whilst that could be the case for a few, the majority must work to sustain and maintain the blessings they have received. This includes increasing your knowledge, network and skill in an ever-evolving environment.

Faith on trial

It's against that backdrop that my entire faith and everything that I believed and held to be true went on trial in 2014. To this day the vivid memory of that season of my life and the impact of my faith took a massive turning point.

We sat poised and waiting for the news in the doctor's office, my younger sister, her mum and our dad. There were only three chairs, so I stood, I mean, I'm not even sure if family groups are permitted to pile into the doctor's office in the way which we did. In the back of my mind, I had braced myself for a little bit of bad news.

The soft-spoken doctor turned to my dad he said in a sombre tone "I'm sorry Mr Mclean the image on the screen that you are looking at, that part shaded in grey is the part where the cancer has spread".

I stepped toward the screen to take a closer look.

"But doctor" I abruptly interrupted "it is grey everywhere" I said half confused and trying to process what this actually means.

At the same time dad was pointing to the parts of his body, elbow, shoulders where he recalled feeling significant pain.

After a moment of silence ensued, which in real terms felt like an eternity, we all sat and processed the meaning of these words that would spin the following five months into a frenzy.

"It is terminal."

"What do you mean? Why did this happen? How did this happen? Are you sure? Have you made a mistake? Are you sure this is his file?

All we could strive to do at this stage was to ensure the remaining 12 months that dad was given were as comfortable, pain-free, and happy as possible, surrounded by family and friends.

I was still in denial, my dad, the great Ras. Seymour Mclean. The Book Liberator, the campaigner of justice. The Self-appointed Ambassador of Ethiopia. The European Consultant, The BS5750 Expert. The Lloyds of London senior Electrical Engineer. My childhood hero, my teenage nemesis, my adult advisor and my mirror was dying.

God, why? God, where are you? God, are you going to heal him? He is a good man. He is selfless, he is only 57. He has spent 30 years of his life committed to social justice for the Rastafarian community. John Dollar had written and produced the gripping 1989 channel 4 production, documenting the trial that would see him spend nine months in Her Majesty's custody for "liberating" over 2,500 books and sending them back to Africa and the Caribbean. Books and relics that he believed did not belong in a British Museum, but rather in the nations from which they were stolen.

For me, the death of a parent is an indescribable pain. You won't know what it feels like until it happens to you. Whilst of course it is a common experience, I learnt that common experiences can have a profound effect.

It launched a period of deep self-reflection and a transformation of my adult identity. How could this even be? We had not lived together since I was five years old. It was as if 39 years of my life I could see the characteristics of my dad in me, I was confused. It was not as if I grew up wanting to be like him. In fact, it was very much the opposite, I didn't think we shared the same values. I grew up thinking about how different we are. But his death caused me to see our similarities, values and imperfections are very aligned. I was even more confused, and now I had questions. God, who will answer these questions?

I was absorbing the parts of my dad that I admired. My missional approach to work and the real-life scenarios that we face in life caused me to think deeper and better understand the tension between the ability to reconcile my faith with my life, livelihood and leadership all whilst running a business.

Through the death of my dad, faith permitted me to better understand the purpose of life, my focus evolved into a personal, generational and eternal perspective.

Life is like a series of personal revelations that impact on your habits and intentions.

Livelihood allows us to explore the seeds that we sow and how we can live out our values with intent in a sustainable eco-system of support.

Legacy reminds me that when we are no longer physically here , we live on in different ways. More recently, I have been speaking with my clients about legacy and estate planning because your treasures are not just for pleasure. I have found that underserved communities talk more than take action on this important topic. Like putting frameworks in place that can guard their legacy.

To mark the 30th year of business, we created a Life Care Plan to support women over 40 in particular to better plan for their health care and social care and create legal and financial plans to support the latter stages of life.

In 2013 Patrick and I had an amazing invitation from our friend Matt Bird an international speaker, author and broadcaster, to join him for a weekend in a monastery. It was incredibly exciting because we had never done anything like this before. In preparation, we were to read Finding Sanctuary, monastic steps for everyday life.

Little did I know at the time, it was soon to become a place of wisdom and insight in helping me to better understand my journey of faith.

Over the last few years, I've come to learn that the way you lead your daily life is key part to finding sanctuary, like the morning routines spoken of in the accountability is key section. It feels like a heightened sense of awareness, slowing down the busyness of life has been key to building my faith and that's one of the key reasons why prayer and meditation at the start of my day is so important for me helping me gain a new perspective and in some cases recuperate.

Ancient Egyptian philosophy teaches why the one who sits in solitude and quiet has escaped from three wars; hearing, speaking and listening. Yet against one thing shall he continually battle that is his own heart.

Finding Sanctuary

I like the way Abbott Christopher Jamison describes the art of discovering meaning. **Reading** as it were, puts food into your mouth **meditation** chews it and breaks it up, and **prayer** extracts its flavour, whilst **contemplation** is the sweetness that refreshes and gladdens. The image of eating is a helpful one, we all do it. As social entrepreneurs, we are driven by a set of values that contribute to a bigger picture, and these moments of reflection help us maintain balance.

We are already convinced that part of the success equation for physical health, emotional health, and mental health lies in basic lifestyle choices. Exercise, prayer, solitude, eating habits, resting habits, recognition that my faith and sensitivity to others and my readiness to live with integrity requires intentionality.

I want my life to be a reflection of hope. The key spiritual resource religion offers is hope. The reasons for living and hoping are the heart of true religion. As I began to better understand the role that faith plays in my life, it's in moments of deepest darkest despair, the death of my father, and the challenges of building an organisation that will be known for its immense contribution to society that I built mustard seed faith.

- What does your faith or values compel you to contribute to society?

LESSON: Mustard Seed Faith

Faith trusts that God will give you what you need to take the next step in order to fulfil your purpose

Chapter 7

Family is priority

I am the proud mother of two incredible children, both fiercely independent, very vocal and opinionated about issues impacting society and the way and how we live. A massive heart for supporting and empowering others.

Patrick and I have tried to be intentional about creating an environment where they could both flourish in their chosen area, extra-curricular activities, educational toys, learning trips and excursions, broad conversations about a range of topics and when it felt like we needed additional input we were not afraid to introduce them to others whose opinions and lifestyle may have been different to ours, but could give them a balanced perspective on life. Like any parent, we wanted to do our best to nurture balanced children. The old African proverb says, "it takes a village to raise a child".

Like many parents, the painful question of, did I do this right? Has plagued my thoughts on many occasions. I have comforted myself by reminding my deepest self that I did the best that I could with the knowledge, energy and resources I had.

Speaking with family and friends with young adult children, I can see the value of intelligent conversations and what these conversations reveal about your child's life experience. To this day, our son, some 22 years later, will tell you that his grandparents had lions in their house in Jamaica. Of course, the small light brown dogs to a two-year-old looked like massive lions, and its bark must have sounded like a loud roar. It is a story that we chuckle at. Every time I remember this I am gently reminded of other precious memories of the innocence and simplicity of the mind of children.

It wasn't until our daughter told me that the business we had created was like the third child in the home that a few alarm bells went off in my head. The conversation caused me to reflect on my parenting style, and I began to do some research about birth order syndrome. As our conversation progressed, she then added that this third child also had additional needs. Her observation implied that I spent more time in my business than with my children. As I began to search for the meaning in her discourse, I began to explore further child birth order syndrome and exactly how this impacts family dynamics but, more importantly, how this is impacting my children's view of me.

Birth order theory is the idea that the order in which a child is born within their family influences their development and personality. The theory was originally introduced by psychotherapist Alfred Adler in the 1920s. Whilst the topic is debated amongst the scientific community, the intersecting factors of environment, context, parental educational attainment and sexuality all play a part in a child's development. I was intrigued to further explore the impact of my parenting style on the development of my children.

In the early stages, I did not realise that I needed to create a structure that needed me less. As any good social entrepreneur would do, I threw myself into the business because, of course, it was the business that was part of our livelihood. It was the vehicle that we used to create massive impact in the community. In 2008 the business was the reason why I received an investiture for services to Social Enterprise at Buckingham Palace. How could I be needed less? But through the eyes of my daughter, the business was taking my attention. At that time, I hadn't recognised the amount of time that I was spending in the business and the view this was forming in the life of my children. I only operated at one speed, which was 100 miles an hour and for as much as I am an organised person, I have an amazing support network. I recognise that I have done and achieved the things I have done because I have an amazing support team.

In Penny Power OBE book "Business is Personal", she cites *"emotional and mental strength governs our success, it's our ability to know ourselves deeply and find emotional strength to overcome mental shocks. I think that starting a business is one of the most Courageous messages that you send to yourself and to the world. It's a message that you send to yourself. You are Resilient No salary will come from anyone. No appraisal will come from anyone, you are the boss it's a giant step".*

For that reason, the third child was taking my attention. In the early days I had not yet fully understood the business ecosystem. I had not yet learnt that the scars of business would contribute to the strength and making of who I was becoming.

Like a baby, a new business requires time, attention and creativity. Building a robust management system, and resilient, flexible and adaptable frameworks took time for me to learn. I learned to build my family life and responsibilities around the requirements of my business. I had a meticulous personal organisational structure. I had planned out the school run, Patrick did the mornings I did the pickups. The office was where schoolwork was completed. After the team left to go home, we left. It was a military operation with allocated time slots that needed to be observed in order to ensure school was not adversely impacted. Then it was bath, supper, reading and bed!

I've often heard it said that your work informs your identity. I now realise that as I had thrown myself into my work, I was shaping the person that I wanted to be. I was shaping the bigger contribution that I wanted to make to the world. Beyond parenting, I was learning how to relate to other people, and other cultures, I was learning to better understand the economy, I was learning to understand the systems of the community, society and its key influences in Government, Education, Media, Arts and Culture Faith and of course family.

Family is the main driver of my legacy and life, the reason why I do what I do. So, when my daughter told me that through her eyes, the business was the third child which required additional attention, I had to rethink my actions and my thoughts. I had to think deeper about my work-life balance and question, does work-life balance even exist?

The conversation with myself about legacy, generational wealth, social mobility and values, runs deep. I recall several key conversations with my Relationology mastermind group and other key influencers in my life about the impact of work life balance and if the concept really does exist. To a certain extent there is an element of obsession if you categorically want to be excellent at something, there will need to be a level of sacrifice and sometimes we choose to make the sacrifice early on so we can reap the benefits later.

Life is somewhat like a relay race, we are passing on a baton to the next generation. The baton represents values, ethics, characteristics, generational wealth and in my case business. What happens to those things will determine the impact of our legacy.

The wise King Solomon in the book of Ecclesiastes said, "there is a time and a season for everything."

I found my work exciting, obsessive and consuming. The conversation about well-being at that point wasn't necessary as far as I was concerned, but what I do know is that well-being is responsible for progress, and running a business is like having another child.

What I do know is the importance of ensuring balance in that space because everyone will be impacted by the lack of it.

It's in my blood

It was not until the death of my amazing grandparents that I recognised a seed of entrepreneurship was sown in my life. I think back to how my grandparents came to the United Kingdom as immigrants in search of opportunities to create a better life for themselves and their children, my parents.

It must have been perplexing to leave your home and country, to migrate to another land in search of something that you don't know even exists based on the promise of a government. I reflect on Nanny McLean working on the London underground. She was able to purchase a four-bedroom house in 1979. I'd love to ask her questions about what drove her tenacity and doggedness to make this happen for herself and her four children without a companion or life partner. I recall wonderful weekends at her beautiful home, it was like a maze. My mum would always pack my weekend case, but I knew that I was guaranteed to return home with more than what I arrived with. I was the first and only grandchild, the first "girl" in the family.

Grandma and grandad Mitchell came to the United Kingdom In the 1960's. Like most Caribbean parents of that era, they would leave the children with trusted family members whilst they went on ahead to pave the way and make sure the country that they were relocating to was fit for the rest of their children. Navigating their way through a system that was not designed to see them flourish they found jobs that enabled them to provide for their family, and live a comfortable life.

It was at the funeral of my grandparents that I really recognised the full extent of their entrepreneurial nature. My grandparents returned to the land of their parents to retire. It was at the funeral that I learnt how my grandad had brought water pipes to the district of Milk River, in Clarendon, in order to ensure everybody else in the area could have running water. His friends would tell me how he had lent "English pounds" to them. English pounds were significant because of the value of the pound at that time..

As I come to a stage in my life where I have to navigate life and legacy, I'm taking my cue from my entrepreneurial grandparents.

The gargantuan life lessons are transformational. When I found myself in life-altering situations and weighty decisions, I leaned into the root of the tenacity, strength, courage and boldness that forms part of my DNA.

Working with my husband

Since 1996 I've had the honour of working with my husband, founding Director and chief visionary of PJs Community Service. Mutual respect forms part of our philosophy for life and marriage. Patrick is one hundred per cent extrovert. A great connector, he is charismatic and a passionate big-picture thinker. He has at least 101 new ideas every morning before 11am. Contrast that with me, the introvert wife. I enjoy solitude, a place to think and create systems and frameworks that strengthen our organisation's impact. We are totally opposite in the way we work, our personality styles are at opposite ends of the spectrum. Yet we share similar values.

We have chosen to make it work because we love each other, and we recognise the unique value that we each bring to our family and business.

Good Relationships don't just happen, they require maintenance. A healthy dose of open, two-way communication, keeps misunderstandings at bay. Plenty of affection and a deep understanding of your spouse's love language. Mutual respect for their contribution and different perspective. I am my husband's biggest cheer leader and critical friend. Challenging him to continuously strive to be the best version of himself, for himself and us. As much as I hate to admit it, I don't always get it right, a positive dose of forgiveness is helpful as I require the same level of grace. Understanding the ability to be flexible enough to see from a different perspective allows the goal and not the role to remain front and centre. Loyalty speaks of trustworthiness and reliability. At regular intervals, Patrick and I take time out for "Marriage Maintenance".

Balancing the changing needs of a growing social enterprise as well as prioritising marriage requires intentionality and focus.

Here are some of my top tips on how you can work with your spouse without divorcing. This has worked for us for over 26 years.

1. **Be clear about your roles and responsibilities.** Be clear about what you each bring to the organisation and who is responsible for each area of the business. Don't allow your differences to divide. Put frameworks in place that will hold you accountable as well as allow for personal and professional growth. These boundaries will help to minimise conflict.
2. **Set work hours/boundaries**. Whilst this may be a challenge initially, especially if you have young children or adult dependants, but creating boundaries around your work hours will allow you to have dedicated time for your relationship, time to focus on each other and what you need outside of the business as well as your own self-care routines.
3. **Imagine you are not working together**. If he/she was not your spouse, how would you respond? This is a

difficult one, but the purpose here is to help you to remain objective as a valuable team player.

4. **Reap the rewards**. If you work hard, I believe it is right that you play hard. Regularly take focussed time to review and celebrate your successes with each other.
5. **Have set business meetings**. Use this as an opportunity to hold each other accountable. Have a set business meeting with an agenda, clear objectives, take notes and assign actions and deadlines, review and evaluate personal performance, in the same way you would if you were working for an organisation that you do not own.
6. **Give each other space**. You are married and live together, take time to breathe away from each other, and develop hobbies and interests outside of the context of your business. Patrick plays tennis, he has his own set of friends that don't involve me. As do I, we meet at regular intervals, we shop, go to the theatre, we travel, we laugh, we cry.
7. **Create a team outside of your family.** I found that because we were both passionate about community transformation and social enterprise, it was important for us to have people on our team that share similar values but come with a different frame of reference, they have helped us to see our blind spots.

LESSON: Family is priority

Never forget the reason why you do what you do. Sometimes we can get lost along the way. In the busyness of life, create space to enjoy quality time with your loved ones.

Chapter 8

Creating Financial Eco-systems

Many people from my parent's generation have grown up with the belief and deception that money is evil. This unfortunate conditioning in some cases, has been passed down to the next generation. I believe that money is a magnifier, it has the ability to amplify the person you already are. Money in and of itself is not evil, it is the love of it that deceives people to do evil things.

> *1 Timothy 6:10 - For the love of money is the root of all evil:*
> *Ecclesiastics 7:12 - For wisdom is a protection even as money is a protection. Money is a defence.*

Money requires responsibility. Having it is one thing, and spending it is another, but your capacity to make it grow is a different type of strategy.

The mindset, strategy and system required to manage a 7-figure business requires a different set of tools and understanding. I realised that what got me to a seven-figure social enterprise would not take me to an eight-figure organisation. I also recognise that my personal financial growth was linked to my business growth. The more I understood money, the more I could create frameworks to acquire it, manage it and make it multiply.

Turning over seven-figures requires strict and meticulous processes to ensure the correct checks and balances are in place. My accountant has always been very key to my business activity in helping me to better understand what the numbers mean and more importantly, how I can ensure the numbers are going in the right direction. This meant having a strong handle on costs as well as income. I saw the practical application of this as I sat on boards with responsibility for millions and the meticulous audit committee meetings that ensured appropriate governance and risk management processes were top priority. I used this as a learning opportunity for my own business to ensure that whatever I was learning that I was able to re-frame it and make it fit for the context of social enterprise and implement it.

Financial Literacy for many social entrepreneurs is not always top of the agenda. In my experience as a mentor, my mentee's priorities are usually built around the social goals and objectives of the organisation. This is usually because there is a skills gap, some do not have access to information and do not know where to go to acquire the information. This, of course comes at a price. That cycle of wanting more but not knowing where to go or how to access the resource in order to make the shifts required.

That is one of the reasons why I am a massive advocate for financial literacy programs in schools. I was commissioned by an organisation to deliver training to a cohort of entrepreneurs. I was really excited because I enjoy seeing other people develop their business ideas. I feel like I am a broker of possibilities, helping others to see possibilities in the face of complex challenges. I diligently prepared PowerPoint slides with real-life examples and case studies to ensure I had effectively taken into consideration the learning styles of the participants. I had prepared group work as well as time for individual reflections on the key points. I prepared implementation tasks for the mentees to apply the learning directly to their own organisations. Then came the jaw-dropping question, "What if I make £100,000 and it turns me into a different person?"

I fully understand that everyone is on their own personal journey, especially as it relates to money and their respective experiences. But for a moment, the question stopped me in my tracks. It reinforced the notion that Michael E Gerber speaks of in his book "The E Myth". People often start their own businesses because they excel at work in a certain sector, such as; a hairdresser, graphic designer, or Social Worker. Then one day, they experience what Gerber refer's to as "*Entrepreneurial Seizure*". The realisation they don't want to do the technical work for someone else. They want to start their own social enterprise, and furthermore they want to develop their own ideas and concepts. The critical assumption and sometimes mistaken belief, is that knowing how to do the technical work is not the same as running a business. Hence the reason why many businesses fail.

According to Small Business Administration, 20% of businesses in the UK fail in the first year, and half fail in the first 5 years, and by year 10, only 33% survive. There are a number of reasons behind these sobering statistics, one being, some people start for the wrong reasons. I see business as a vehicle for social change, social mobility, job creation and community wealth building. This means considering a future-focused approach that far exceeds your individual capabilities and more about the strength of the team whilst increasing your capacity for more.

This observation also served to remind me that people do things for different reasons, and as a good mentor and trainer, my responsibility is to demonstrate the art of the possible and to explain that £100,000 for example, is just the start. There are much more opportunities beyond the £100,000 milestone.

Creating a personal financial eco-system requires preparation and focus with a strategic and deliberate approach. The purpose of the system is to lay out a framework to advance your personal financial well-being, taking into account the factors that influence your current position. Once you have some clarity, you are then able to design a methodology that marries your expectations, taking into consideration the educational and behavioural influences, interventions and efforts that you can realistically achieve in a given timeframe.

These foundational factors may be responsible for defining your personal journey reflecting on your basic education, skills, and abilities around numeracy, problem-solving, and critical thinking. This includes the way you process information, your understanding of the general economic conditions, the socioeconomic factors, your personal health, your family experiences and cultural factors that need to be considered. Also important are the economic inequalities and social welfare that you may have been exposed to. These comprise the basic educational understanding and foundational factor that will support your understanding of creating an eco-system.

The gap created will allow you to implement the next phase of where you want to get to and to close that gap using the knowledge and skills acquired to access the next most feasible and affordable steps. Heavily influenced by your circle of influence including coaches, mentors, advisors and teachers they have the capacity to affect the pathway you create which will ultimately impact your financial outcomes. Have you heard the saying *"if you hang out with rich people, you will be richer, even by reason of the types of conversations that you are exposed too. When you hang out with winners, they want to see you win also"*.

The strategy shared by George Clason in his book "the Richest Man in Babylon" gives insight into managing your finances. As I reframed the principles for my personal progress during the most challenging seasons of my life, I have experienced how these same principles have lifted me out of awkward situations and near financial ruin.

1. Don't eat your seed

The concept of living on 70% of your income requires discipline. I learnt this concept whilst at university. Coming from a home that didn't have much surplus cash, I was always mindful that I might need some money for that rainy day. I recall conversations with mum about money and the lack of it. As a teenager, I learnt very quickly that if bills are not paid, there are consequences. The breakdown of my mum's marriage and the subsequent non-payment of the mortgage led to our family home being repossessed. Something was planted in me that said if I had enough money, then perhaps I could position myself so that if I ever needed anything in life, I would have the means or be resourceful enough to locate it. With that backdrop, in 1994, I started my first Saturday job in Ravels shoe shop. I think my love of shoes was birthed on my first day on the shop floor. Louder than my love of shoes was the voice of my mother reminding me not to spend all my hard earn cash on the mandatory monthly pair of new shoes. So, I decided to pluck a figure out of the air £5.00 was good and started saving £5 per week. That was a huge amount of money for a 15 year old school girl, but it taught me a rhythm and made me realise that the first person that I had to pay was "myself". When my statement would arrive the sheer joy of seeing my money accumulate, made me feel like a gardener growing seeds. I could see growth and growth birthed excitement. I was learning not to eat my seed.

2. Be disciplined about your expenses

A budget is a control mechanism not a punishment. I believe that money requires a mission, your pounds must have a purpose, dollars need direction or the pressure of life will consume your income and before you know it you will have nothing.

The purpose of the budget is to help you colour within the lines of your financial capabilities. It decides if you can go on holiday and where you go, buy that car, upgrade your property, send the children to private school or extra curricula activities. Your ability to budget will encourage you to forecast and put strategies in place to structure for increase, because your audacious goals and dreams also require a financial plan. In the same way that organisations decide based on the budget we can or can't.

Managing your emotions is an important part of financial management. Not allowing greed or lust to cause you to live outside of your means. Learning to live within your means is an emotional journey. On a personal level I had this on lock. On a business level I had to learn the hard way. Having an accountant helped to keep in check my expenditure. The challenge however are the unexpected situations, like, death or that leaking roof or the broken washing machine. That is why the first 10% that you didn't spend will come in handy.

3. Make your money work

I enjoyed seeing my money accumulate, it gave me a sense of freedom, security, opportunity and access. Money gives you options. It gave me the ability to serve others and I could see myself growing through this process. I needed to find a way to make the little that I have multiple in a way that would impact the social mobility of my family and also generate wealth. Coming from my background I was risk averse, I didn't realise that in order for my money to grow, I needed to put my money to work. There are many options, and you have to take professional guidance on which method is best for you. Property investments, Stock Markets, and Precious metals, all of which have an element of risk associated, but I couldn't bear the thought of losing not even one pence that I had worked so diligently for. That is why the second 10% will be useful for investment, allowing you to leverage opportunities at the appropriate time.

4. Protect your Money from loss

Security systems to protect your wealth are just as paramount as generating money in the first place. My husband coined the phrase, *"If you hang with turkeys, you will be dead by Christmas"*. I'll add that if you live in the USA, you have until Thanksgiving.

The phrase speaks of the network of people you take advice from. It is important to speak with experts. Guarding your money is just as important as making your money. Guarding your money, among other things, includes insurance options, pensions, Lasting Power of Attorney and Trusts, of course, there are other options and other routes. Focus on what is right for you and your family at this moment in time. As you increase your capacity, you may require a more robust system.

5. Make your house profitable

My amazing Grandmother, affectionately known as Nanny, taught me the value of property ownership. Nanny purchased her property in 1979 a four-bedroom house in South West London, for approximately £5,000. Back then, the implication of her tenacity and sheer determination didn't really mean much to me. It wasn't until I began to develop my own property portfolio that I realised the power of her actions. I was viewing now through the lens of an adult the lessons I had missed as a child. The leverage that owning a property gives is incredible. It was unfortunate that my community did not always have access to this information, but she demonstrated that as a single woman, savvy and focused on the future, how to leverage opportunities. She taught me that owning a property gives you options to leverage.

6. Ensure an income for your future

Pension plans, Lasting Power of Attorney, and Life insurance. It's important to know about structures and implement them to protect your wealth and that of your family and posterity. These were not common conversations in my family. Still, as I was determined to increase my capacity for more, I was resolute and intentional about putting myself in places where I could learn more, be more and ultimately do more.

I was first inspired by my client Mrs Connell, her solicitor had lasting power of Attorney over her estate, which meant they were responsible for her health and finances. Given that she was 88 years old, she needed someone to manage her affairs. Our organisation provided care for her 24 hours a day over a ten year period. Costing approximately £6,000 per month, £72,000 per year, that's over £750,000 in care costs. The real question is, what eco-system did she create in order to ensure her later years would be comfortable?

7. Increase your ability to Earn

To be wise, it is important to study wise people. Wisdom speaks of your ability to apply knowledge to a situation, it has everything with your ability to perceive or sense a situation. Wisdom and experience cannot be taught, but opportunities for learning and practising sound judgement can be created.

I had to find a way to increase my ability to earn. I can recall some childhood memories. It was a common conversation in our circles that if you wanted to progress, you had to work twice as hard as your non-black counterparts. Money was tight, and I had a mission, so I started investing in myself by buying books. I could see the evidence of my increase through my language and my thinking capacity. This led to bigger and better opportunities. The opportunities brought me to different spaces, with different people and new conversations, I was constantly learning. I could feel my appetite had changed and I wanted more. I started attending conferences and taking copious notes. I would read and re-read the notes for days and intentionally and consciously make the strategic shifts required. It felt like as I pushed myself, more doors of opportunity would open. Each door came with a new set of requirements, new learning, new people, new access and new challenges.

Sometimes we are unconsciously blinded by our circumstances. It is all we have known to be true, and it is all we have been exposed to. Growing up in marginalised circumstances has the capacity to trap you into a single narrative without recognising that the single narrative is only one perspective. Given that in 2019 there are approximately 66 million people in the United Kingdom, not to mention eight billion people in the entire world, each with a different outlook on life. The unspoken interpretation of these important statistics reminds us that there is always another perspective that is likely to be different for our own.

- Use the points listed above to get yourself started and ask yourself:
- What do you want your financial status to look like 3 years from now?

LESSON: Creating Financial Eco-systems

Money needs a mission or purpose.

It needs a robust system for acquisition, management and distribution.

Chapter 9

Define your fun

What is your definition of fun?

I struggled with this because I didn't really have a clear concept of what fun was meant to be. I believe I was trying to fit into someone else's definition – not realising that I could create my own framework for what I wanted fun to be.

It's almost like when people say, "let's go out for a fun night out", for me a fun night our is curled up on my sofa with a good book a cup of hot water with lemon and a bag or two of sweet and salted popcorn. Or if Patrick is home both our legs entwined whilst watching a good movie enjoying each other's company. I appreciate that for some that might be the height of boredom.

I am an introvert, extremely comfortable being on my own. I tend to focus on my inner thoughts and ideas, and reflections help me to evaluate and monitor my progress and prepare for how I can improve myself to be the best version I can be.

Like most introverts, I am reserved and calm, I tend to be rigid as I usually would have set up a plan that, in my opinion, needs to be enacted.

This was the hardest chapter to write because, in my mind, I knew that I didn't fit the conventional definition of fun. For most, fun is about people, experience, memories, amusement, enjoyment, pleasure, and deep belly laughs. Whilst I had all of those things, there was a huge disconnect.

At this age and stage of life, I want to capture moments. Moments create meaningful memories, bringing great joy. It is important to capture these meaningful memories as it creates muscle memory, trophies and souvenirs to point towards when life gets tough.

This is very different to when I was in my thirties. I wanted to be out with friends or business associates, building and growing. Attending conferences, building my network travelling.

As I get older, there is a compelling desire to create more memories. I have realised that in your forties, you tend to care less about the opinions of others and more about the impact you can have in the world. We often talk about the dash in between the time you are born and the time you depart this earth and what you want that dash to represent.

In 2021 I wanted to immortalise and capture the essence of fun as well as do something that I had never done before in order to stretch myself. With me, there always has to be a bigger rationale. One of the rare occasions that I would focus entirely on me enjoying the moment and creating memories.

I carefully curated a team that would help me achieve this goal as I had zero idea of what this would entail, I just knew I wanted to capture something different. I had no idea of the preparation required vocal exercise and the process of laying a track. Even though we use to own a community facility that housed several music studio's, I had never ventured in to using them, I was usually focused on business.

Ryan, my younger brother and vocal coach, helped me prepare. I was secretly excited and nervous at the same time as I could see my idea coming together. The other thought I had to get my head around is that I was doing this for fun. Some people actually do this to make a living and generate income. Ryan is a soulful R&B singer, songwriter and musician. He has worked with some amazing artists, including Stormzy, Childish Gambino, Tom Grennan, Emile Sandé, Kano, Shalamar, the legend Elton John as well as jazz legend Roy Ayers. He has opened up for Grammy Award-winning American artist PJ Morton, as well as soul and R&B greats Eric Roberson and Teedra Moses. With this level of experience I knew I was in good hands. Whilst I was looking for fun, he was serious about making sure my vocals were ready for the world stage.

Velroy Bailey had the musical arranging expertise I needed. I actually didn't have a clue about this project, he came with world-class arrangements, he has played on some of the world's biggest and best stages with the likes of the Jackson Five, Drifters Tour, Simply Red, Blue, Alexander Burke, Kingdom Choir and a range of Britain's got talent show finalists. Having this level of expertise on my project exposed me to a different level of excellence. This was exciting watching my idea come to fruition.

It was awe-inspiring watching my creative director breathe life into my project. I saw how he mimed the words of the song and brought to life the imagery that supports the storyline. Antonio Lewis employed a holistic and media-centric approach, he created, a bespoke plan paying close attention to the overall goal, audience and message.

My award-winning stylist and fashion designer, Jeanette Young, made me look and feel like some kind of celebrity. Having worked in the fashion industry for over 15 years as a consultant for most of the high street brands. One of Jeanette's highlights was styling The Kingdom Choir for the royal wedding of Prince Harry and Meghan Markle, which gained over 3 billion views because of their grand performance and their elegant, glamorous look. I was delighted that she was on my team.

My glam squad consisted of hair stylist Aaron Hill and makeup artist Bukkiah Param together they ensured the glamorous look was maintained for the entire day. Whilst I was living one of my dreams and having fun, they were busy working to ensure that I could have fun.

Behind the scenes, Kimberley Lawson my personal photographer captured the moment that would help to encapsulate this day in history and of course she took some footage for social media.

One of the incredible lessons from my fun project was the importance of having great people on your team. I had world-class creatives helping me bring a fun project to life. The process of dreaming and planning and execution has so many facets, and even though I had been running a business my entire working life, I was learning a new level of excellence and the layering process of creativity. A process of which I had applied to my business for years - but this was new. Whilst I was having fun, the team were busy working and ensuring everything was captured perfectly. The missed kissing scene when our lips didn't collide, I actually didn't want to smudge my lipstick. The walk that made me look like I was actually falling down the elegant staircase was all part of memory-making.

https://www.youtube.com/watch?v=YyOt84Eex38 Here is the link to the youtube music video. This song, Everlasting Love tells a story of the strength of hope, courage and faith in the middle of feeling despair, doubt and anxiety. It speaks of my personal journey of having a life-altering Breast Cancer diagnosis in 2019, catapulting my mind into the deepest level of anguish that I had ever felt and how having my husband and best friend in my life that you could lean on helped to pull me through some of the darkest days. I wanted to demonstrate my gratitude in an artistic way.

I created and captured my version fun. I have left-brain tendencies and had to process fun in a way that made sense to me. I have come to process in boxes in order to help me create systems. To better help me define the type of fun that I was searching for, I turned to the gamification framework, because this process uses game mechanics, modules and principles, applying them to a non-game context. In Nicole Lazzaro's theory of fun, she states that there are four different kinds of fun that are general categories that appear in any kind of game-like context (Werbach, 2013)

Each of the four types of fun reveal different types of player experiences. Nicole Lazzaro states that games that use emotions from four types of interactions are more likely to capture attention and motivate play. These are:

Hard Fun – the goal is to ascertain a level of mastery. This is about winning, overcoming challenges, defeating obstacles, creating strategies and moving up levels. I love this concept because in my organisation I have spent a significant chuck of my career learning to overcome challenges through the highs and low of the journey. The number of times that I have had to dig deep within myself to find a solution in order to move. In life, I am faced with what appears to be the biggest challenge of my life, and now I need to find a solution. Could it be that my life and business experience prepared me for this moment?

Easy Fun – the drive is about tapping into the imagination, exploring concepts, interpreting information, investigating options, getting creative and figuring things out. This is not my strong point; my children will loudly confirm this. I work at my own pace and don't want to be boxed in or have to conform to the expected norms and behaviours of others. The escape room experience highlighted this for me.

People Fun – seeks to work with others in co-operation, competing, using all forms of communication, to enhance your performance, this deepens the personal experience. I have spent my entire career developing people fun. As a business leader, I can only construct and co-create concepts that impact our future with people. As a leader, I have observed first-hand the generational impact this can have.

Serious Fun - linked to life and values, for example, meditation, working out at the gym, learning new things, completing a challenge – this, to me, represents personal mastery and development. This is one of the reasons why I really enjoyed going to the gym at 5.30am or the 6am prayer call or learning new processes to enhance my quality of life, serious fun. This causes me to look deeper into myself and pull together all the facets of fun that will permit me to be me.

I wanted a mixture of all of these things, and in order to arrive at that point, I needed to create a strategy that directly addressed the areas of my deficiency.

During this process of exploration, I realised it is important to capture memories. Memories are like trophies or souvenirs, you are able to point to them as significant achievements and monuments of your past that create the tapestry of life. As we create the tapestry of life, we are constantly making shifts and adjusting through the transitions, leaving one chapter, while moving on to another, all the while strengthening your character and the frame of who you are.

I have learnt through this process that I cannot be afraid of the transition. It is easy to feel secure in a pond or in a smaller space, but if you never venture out, you will never know that there is an ocean of possibilities and opportunities. Transition is a journey, it is filled with new discoveries for the individual.

I created my own rhythm and definition of fun. I consistently want to develop mastery and contribute to my values through relationships. I also acknowledge that balance is key. Having good people and secure, strong people in my life, my husband is this, he helps me not to miss out on the important things, he covers my short-sightedness, the things that I don't see as important, and he presents a different perspective, and that contributes to my personal growth.

Friends with Faith

It is important to have friends that are a little like the character Joy from the 2015 Pixar animated movie Inside Out. The character Joy was depicted by a bright yellow character with blue hair full of energy and life. Always wanting to bring happiness and delight to the situation, sometimes to the detriment of reality.

As a business leader, I believe it is important to surround yourself with friends like Joy. Thought leaders and those with a growth mindset, those that can bring joy when your own happiness feels like it has gone on a long journey. Around 10 years ago I championed the organising of our first mastermind group with a group of friends. Each of us were on a different business trajectory with incredible skill set, mindset and heart set to achieve remarkable things in our respective areas of influence.

The other incredible reality is that each of us were experiencing, considerable personal life challenges, loss, divorce, liquidation. These real-life issues have the capacity to take a toll on your emotional, mental and spiritual well-being. Nevertheless, every month we met without fail, and we treated ourselves to classy restaurants and comfortable surroundings. We spoke about business growth and development and how we would intentionally increase our capacity for more over the four-week period before our next meeting. It breathed life into our challenges. It reinforced the conversation around your network being your net worth.

One of the key lessons during this period was the recognition that we all had personal life challenges. But our monthly restaurant meetings gave us strength, something fun to look forward to and to push through loss, grief, pain, and health challenges. We had the capacity to inject the joy and fun back into each other.

Having family and friends around me at key moments of life sometimes feels like the wind beneath my wings. Their words gave me strength, courage and built my fortitude. Their words have the power to assist me and maintain focus and not to lose sight of the bigger picture.

My friends and family showed up in full strength in the run-up to surgery. I told some key individuals about the cancer diagnosis. I was already aware of how important it was to insulate myself with positivity. In the same way carpet provides insulation for a room, helping to save energy, it is an important contributor to the insulation of the indoor environment. Carpet insulates floors as it provides a psychological feeling of warmth. In the same way, my friends and relatives did when they came to the house to lift my spirits, sharing love, warmth and strength in my lowest moment. On this particular occasion I'm convinced I cried, curled up in the foetal position for ten minutes but Patrick tells me in was more like 45 minutes. Whatever the timeframe the real point here is who are your friends? Do they have the ability to speak life over your circumstances? Do your friends have the discerning ability to look past what the eyes can see?

On a practical level, sending cards, flowers, fruit baskets, text messages and WhatsApp messages are incredible gestures that have the power to boost your mental health. If ever there was a seed of doubt or discouragement, the visual display of gifts is evidence that the social group to which you belong care, the sense of belonging is vital for psychological well-being. This contributes to the feeling of care, fun and the sense of belonging that is vital to your personal and professional advancement.

- What is your definition of fun?
- How do you ensure this is an integral part of your everyday life?

LESSON: Define your fun

Once you have decided what you want fun to look like, make it an integral part of life, and you will learn new skills in the process.

Chapter 10

Be ready

Life can be unpredictable; at the best of times, we are navigating a volatile, uncertain, complex and ambiguous environment. Enjoy the moment but don't get too comfortable. Be ready to change.

Your personal story and experience is what will differentiate you from the crowd. Use your story to delve deeper into the insights that you have learnt.

Use your story to ask probing questions of yourself and others and be ready to answer the hard question. Probing questions engender clarification on a matter, for example you could ask "Could you tell me more about that?" or "What are our options if?" or "Are there any potential difficulties if we ...?"

Use your story to explore another context, for example, if the circumstances were different, what could the outcome look like, dream outside of the box.

Give yourself permission to examine a different perspectives, this will stretch your thinking capacity and cause you to ask more questions.

I recall in my role as chair of governors, my role was to act as a critical friend to the headteacher, asking questions that would stretch and challenge the strategic direction of the organisation. This was something I also adopted in my management meetings with my teams and across my stakeholder groups.

The inquisitive mind asks questions. It's the constant message I give to my senior team; "Ask more Questions" it will keep you in the position of a lifelong learner, a student of life. We live in an era where things are changing rapidly. It only feels like yesterday that I brought my babies home in a car chair from the hospital, and now 20 something years later, they have graduated from university, and they're starting their careers.

Medical journals tell us we only use approximately 10% of our brain capacity. This was also depicted in Lucy, the 2014 movie starring Morgan Freeman and Scarlet Johanson. A famous quote from the movie; *"Time is the only true unit of measure. It gives proof to the existence of matter. Without time, we don't exist"*

Over the last few years, I have had the opportunity to really make an assessment of time and understand how important time really is. I found a way to intentionally apply this concept of time to my life. I desire for my life to be meaningful. This means that I must use my 168-hour (7 days a week) allocation of time per week in a productive way.

After having a Mastectomy and treatment for breast cancer in December 2019, time took on a whole new meaning. I felt like I had been given another chance at life. Time was already meaningful, but now it took on a whole new meaning, almost like I just couldn't waste any time. If it didn't sit well with my values, ethics or moral code, I didn't give it much attention. If it didn't give me great joy, or a sense of fulfilment of purpose, it had no place on my radar. I used to wonder if I was at this place because of my age, and I concluded, in your 40's life has a different meaning to your 20's.

In my forties I am way more focused and intentional about what I do. I am less focussed on the trophies of life or how many followers or friends I have on social media. I am more interested and committed to transformation, empowerment and adding value.

I even became fanatical about colour coding my diary so I could see where my time was going, I started reading and researching all sorts of tools to help me better manage my time.

I created the habit tracker. You can download your free copy at www.claudinereidmbe.com

The habit tracker was designed to help you create better personal habits. I intentionally created a simple, user-friendly printable tracker PDF in its first phase to move away from screen time and create thinking and downtime for you.

I started reading up about strategies I could adopt in order to improve my productivity, increase my output and maintain my focus.

I found the Pomodoro Technique, developed by Francesco Cirillo in the late 1980s, to be a real game changer. I have slightly adjusted it to use my own style and discipline. The technique uses a timer to break work into intervals, traditionally 25 minutes in length, separated by short breaks. I started to use my work intervals in 45-minute blocks and take a 15-minute break. My productivity went off the scales! I would set the timer on my mobile phone. I could zone out from all distractions whilst I focused on the task at hand. For those tasks that I really disliked, for example, my filing, I would dedicate a shorter amount of time, but the principle was the same.

I was motivated by the bite-size achievable process that I had worked out. Now the next hurdle to master was the discipline to see it through.

The moral of the story is that I had become more self-aware. I am clear on my drivers and how to get the best out of myself. I know what music to listen to in order to lift my spirits, and I know how to enlist others to support me in the development of minimising procrastination and increasing my productivity. This is a skill I continue to apply in every area of my life and thoroughly recommend.

KEY POINTS

- Knowing yourself is key to progress.
- Having cheerleaders contributes to progress.
- Developing a personal discipline routine is growth.
- Creating the right environment in your head, heart, mind and soul is key for balance. Robin Sharma author of The Monk who sold his Ferrarri introduced me to the concept of balance in this way. Often, we focus on mindset only, however, in order to navigate life, an element of balance is required.

Your story and your experience counts for much. It's your call to decide how much of your personal life you want to share. I have also learnt that it is because of my life experience, my values, my goals, passion and purpose that I am able to encourage, enable and empower others using the vehicle of the eco-system I call social entrepreneurship.

Chapter 11

Navigating Life

Whilst in recovery mode from surgery, I launched my mentoring business, and I created the Life Framework Wheel. Even though I was not able to physically go back to my social enterprise, I was able to work from home at a pace that was conducive to my recovery.

The mentorship concept was designed to support ambitious, entrepreneurial women planning for important areas of life and creating a roadmap for success.

The Life Framework Wheel (see diagram 1) shows how the key areas of life are interlinked. The objective is to set a key goal in each key area of life and design a road map for the achievement of that goal with a set timeframe.

The goal has a direct link to the life, livelihood, leadership and legacy of its creator and will support the owner on the road to navigating life.

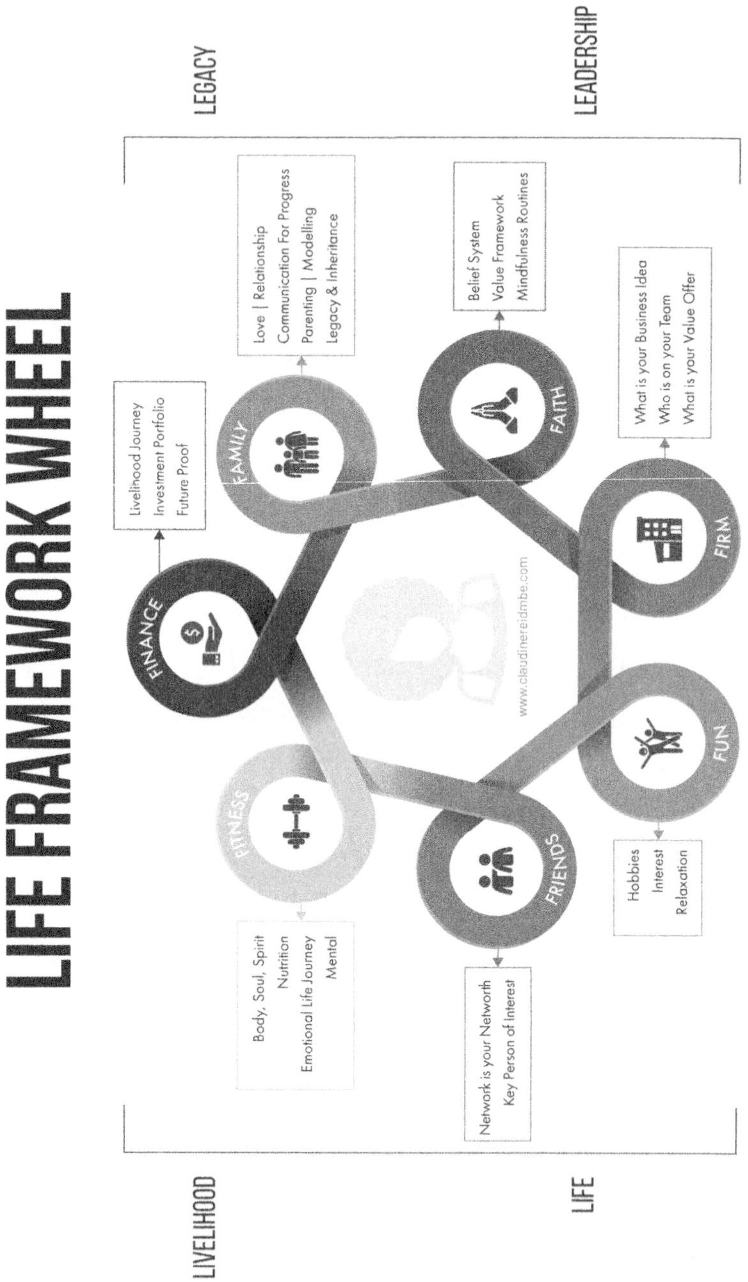
LIFE FRAMEWORK WHEEL
LEGACY
LEADERSHIP
LIVELIHOOD
LIFE
FINANCE
Livelihood Journey
Investment Portfolio
Future Proof
FAMILY
Love | Relationship
Communication For Progress
Parenting | Modelling
Legacy & Inheritance
FAITH
Belief System
Value Framework
Mindfulness Routines
FIRM
What is your Business Idea
Who is on your Team
What is your Value Offer
FUN
Hobbies
Interest
Relaxation
FRIENDS
Network is your Networth
Key Person of Interest
FITNESS
Body, Soul, Spirit
Nutrition
Emotional Life Journey
Mental
www.claudinereidmbe.com

The Navigating Life platform

Created in response to the 2020 Global Pandemic. I head up the women's department at my church and was responsible for leading the wholistic development program for over 500 women.

We shifted our activity onto the virtual space and created a 12-week program that would encourage women with a program of mental health and personal development support for the members.

The 12-week program turned into a 104-week program. Now, after 2 years, it has been revised into a monthly empowerment class. Covering areas of personal, professional and spiritual development for women worldwide, with over 1,000 registered attendees.

It was during one of these sessions that I was inspired to create an anthology. The ambition was to create a space for other women to share their stories of how they had navigated a challenging season in their life I wanted the women to be in a position to inspire other women with stories and messages of hope.

I'm super excited to share with you that 37 women have contributed to the Navigating Life Anthology series. We launched three books over a 13 month period, all of which have made it the Amazon Best seller list.

I've come to realise it's the messenger that makes the message unique and as ambassadors of hope, the women who have written these stories are sharing messages of hope, transformation, determination, and sagacity.

- Ask yourself the question?
- Do you have a story of hope?
- Do you have a story of how you have had to navigate a season in your life?

- Perhaps it's time to take the first step in increasing your capacity for more and allow others to see and to hear the transformation.

Chapter 12

Courage Pledge

As you transition into a new space, mentally take note that in order for this season to be different, something more is going to be required. As you make a quantum leap to truly live, you have a choice.

Courage is a choice

You can either be paralysed by fear and trepidation of the unknown or choose to live.

8 tips for courageous living

1) Don't Panic

Fear of the unknown has the capacity to paralyse your actions. In the moment, a logical approach serves you well. Can you recall a time when you were shocked into paralysis. You wanted to move but your body was not following the instructions from your temporarily anaesthetised brain. It helps to remain calm, and focused, the total opposite is the reality but if you can, find it within yourself. It's almost like you have to focus yourself to dig deep, and then take in another deep breath to pull yourself through.

2) Gain situational awareness / develop your perspective

Perspective is everything. A different perspective allows you to see from someone else's point of view. In business, I tried to adopt the ability to see from my different stakeholder's perspectives, as trying as this may seem, it certainly helped to manage relationships.

I remember when Patrick and I were convinced our bank manager was going to throw the book at us for a few poor financial management decisions that had the potential to have an adverse impact on the business. But we decided ahead of the meeting that if we were the bank manager, what would we want from our client?

The answer was a detailed action plan with regular milestone checks and a contingency plan. This allowed us to ask different questions and create thinking strategies linked with responding to financial risk management, which the bank manager would be concerned about. Thinking about this perspective beforehand put us in a strong solution-focused position. When we entered the room we were able to demonstrate that success is in the preparation. The meeting had a positive outcome, thankfully.

3) Take a mental inventory

Say no to toxic poor habits. Say yes to mental strength-building habits like going to bed at a certain time or only limiting yourself to one slice of cake or keeping the promises that you make to yourself. I learnt to develop this because, in business, I had no one to fall back on. I had to make it work. Sometimes with the tears rolling down my eyes and the ever-present fear of failure, I built mental strength in the tough times.

4) Develop a Victor's mindset

I'm a big believer in self-talk. Self-talk gives me the opportunity to silence the voice of the inner critic and talk back with authority. I am a key player in determining my destiny. That means sometimes my mind will make fear based or limited knowledge-based suggestions, that I have to combat. I've found that physically looking to my left gives me strength, and here is why. In my office on the window ledge, I've created a mini wall of fame. The trophies represent hard work and credibility given by others it directly reminds me that I worked hard to get here.

5) Trust your training

All world-class Olympians know that success is in the preparation. They know what counts. It's the endless hours of training and the muscle memory they have developed that they have to pull on.

People used to ask me why I read so many books. I would always give the same response; I'm training my brain to increase its capacity for more. They would ask how I remember everything. Incredibly, I didn't feel like I remembered a thing until someone asked me a question. It was then that I could feel my brain, like a filing system, searching through the books I had read to give an answer. I trusted that my training would help me most when I needed it.

6) Bend don't break

I remember when I was younger, I always wondered how trees swayed in the wind. They have deep roots. The roots allow the tree to maintain stability and depth, especially in rough seasons. This is the difference between being flexible and adaptable. Allow yourself to be flexible AND adaptable.

7) Learn from the past

My mum always said, *"a wise person learns from other people's mistakes"*. I have tried to apply this concept to business by learning from others that are ahead of me. We don't have to repeat the same errors; learn from them and go again. When people around you act a certain way, believe this is how they will act with you. Study and observe their trends, numbers and behaviour. What gets measured gets managed. You are then able to take corrective action.

8) Help others

I find pleasure in serving others, helping them come to the knowledge of who they are and what they bring to the table. In my most challenging times I help others and it takes the focus off my own situations. This point comes with a warning; it is very easy to bury yourself in service without facing your own demons on the premise that we are doing good work. But hurting people hurt others. Help others, but make sure you help yourself. Sometimes it is necessary to stop and take our own advice.

Activity Checklist

Mind your business

What is the current stage of your Business?

What strategy do you need to employ to increase your weekly or monthly turnover by £2,000?

What strategy do you need to employ to increase your weekly or monthly turnover by £5,000?

What strategy do you need to employ to increase your weekly or monthly turnover by £10,000?

What strategy do you need to employ in order to increase the social or environmental impact?

Identify 5 people that are doing what you would like to do and connect with them in the next 5 days.

Beyond the comfort zone

What parts of your life motivate you to be all you can be, and how will this impact on your leadership ability?

How will this impact your health?

How will this impact your ability to move out of your comfort zone?

Race, Identity & Role Models

Are you able to identify who are the significant contributors to your life and what role they play and why?

The F word

What life lessons has failure taught you and why?

Accountability is key

What frameworks of accountability do you hold yourself to?

Mustard seed Faith

What does your faith or values compel you to contribute to society?

How do you ensure you are able to achieve this?

Family is priority

How do you divorce proof your key relationships?

Creating financial eco-systems

What do you want your financial status to look like 3 years from now?

How are you going to get there?

Define your fun

What is your definition of fun?

How do you ensure this is an integral part of your everyday life?

Claudine Reid MBE

MY MISSION IS TO CREATE MORE LEADERS

Social Entrepreneur, Mentor, Director of Women's Ministry, wife and mother. Claudine is passionate about supporting and bringing out the best in women. She has more than 25 years of experience co-directing an award-winning, 7- figure social enterprise. Her expertise in growing people's talents, organisational development, and motivating others to develop successful habits make her a unique, passionate and inspirational leader and consultant.

Claudine works with social entrepreneurs and influencers, creating an ecosystem of support across key disciplines. Her organisation has employed over 9,000 people, delivering essential services to vulnerable adults and children; Claudine has designed several mentorship programs for entrepreneurs on practical and transformational community impact.

She has drawn on the United Nations' 17 sustainable goals as a catalyst to contribute to a values-driven approach to improving an ecosystem of support for women.

Claudine is a former UK Government Cabinet Office advisor; she currently chairs the Lloyds Banking Group Advisory Committee, supporting the Bank to better understand the challenges and barriers experienced by Black entrepreneurs.

Claudine has been referred to as a life strategist, creating tools and resources that support the personal, professional and spiritual development and journey of women to increase their capacity for more.

www.ClaudineReidMBE.com

Mentorship for Social Entrepreneurs

I'm offering you a proven strategy to strengthen your life roadmap and maximise the potential of your social enterprise. In just 3 months, you can gain financial and business confidence, clarify your purpose with an intentional plan and learn how to balance key priorities in your life

Are you interested?

Visit
www.ClaudineReidMBE.com

The Navigating Life Anthology Series

Available on Amazon and Kindle Worldwide

PJs Community Service

PJ's Community Services is a multi award-winning Social Enterprise, established in 1992 with a focus on Community transformation.

PJ's delivers its mission by providing:
Care and support to Vulnerable Adults and Children's Residential Homes & Semi-Independent Homes
Education & Support to young people that are at risk of exclusion the support is also extended to their families

Social Enterprise Support to organisations, groups and individuals
For more information about visit:
www.PJsGroup.co.uk

Divine Flow Publishing

Publishing People of Influence
onto Platforms for Impact.

The Lord gives the word [of power];
the women who bear and publish [the news]
are a great host. Psalm 68:11 AMPC

www.DivineFlowPublishing.com

Printed in Great Britain
by Amazon

86463629R00081